real
delegation

real
delegation

how to get people to do things for you – and do them well

JK SMART

Prentice
Hall
BUSINESS

An imprint of Pearson Education

London • New York • Toronto • Sydney • Tokyo • Singapore • Hong Kong • Cape Town
New Delhi • Madrid • Paris • Amsterdam • Munich • Milan • Stockholm

PEARSON EDUCATION LIMITED

Head Office:
Edinburgh Gate
Harlow CM20 2JE
Tel: +44 (0)1279 623623
Fax: +44 (0)1279 431059

London Office:
128 Long Acre
London WC2E 9AN
Tel: +44 (0)20 7447 2000
Fax: +44 (0)20 7447 2170
Websites: www.business-minds.com
www.yourmomentum.com

First published in Great Britain in 2003

© Pearson Education Limited 2003

The right of JK Smart to be identified as author of this work has been asserted
by her in accordance with the Copyright, Designs and Patents Act 1988.

ISBN 0 273 66322 4

British Library Cataloguing in Publication Data
A CIP catalogue record for this book can be obtained from the British Library

Transferred to digital print on demand, 2005

Designed by Claire Brodmann Book Designs, Lichfield, Staffs
Typeset by Northern Phototypesetting Co. Ltd, Bolton

Printed and bound by Antony Rowe Ltd, Eastbourne

The Publishers' policy is to use paper manufactured from sustainable forests.

To Mirabella, whose prayers brought me
a much needed miracle.

With thanks to Neil Finn and
Crowded House for providing
the soundtrack to the writing.

Contents

PART 2
Getting delegation right in the *real* world

PART 3
Knowing when to step in and when to stand back 99

Conclusion 129

Appendices 135

About the author

Karen Smart's background is in individual and organizational development. However, unlike some in her field, first and foremost Karen sees herself as a line manager. In recent years, she's worked primarily on enabling managers to manage – developing and delivering everything from individual skill building and management development programmes to management systems design and organization wide culture change. In addition to managing her team, Karen has coached senior managers and facilitated cross-functional working, problem solving and conflict management. Although she has two degrees and has researched extensively across a range of disciplines, ultimately Karen feels she's learned most about management from her experience as an overworked and undervalued manager, disempowered by bureaucracy. From this experience – and inspired by the man she says 'puts the J into JK Smart and a lot of the smart too' – the philosophy of *real* management for *real* people was born.

■ *real* management for the way it is ■

Introduction to *real* management

▶ Welcome to the *real* world

Do you read most management books and say, 'If only it was that easy in the real world'? *Real* management is the answer for every manager who knows it's about doing the best we can with what we've got, in the real world of organizations that are demanding more and more for less and less. It's for real managers who think the books we've read must have been written by people who don't live in our world and who mistake us for superheroes. We know we could work out a better way of managing if only we could get off the treadmill long enough to find the time.

▶ Telling it like it is

But what if someone had read everything, tried everything, worked out why things don't work in the real world, found a way of managing that works with the complexity of real life instead of pretending it's simple, and then taken time off from managing to tell you about it? And what if that someone wasn't a guru, academic or consultant but an ordinary, overworked manager who knows what managers are up against and who doesn't judge or preach or try to get people to be something they're not? And what if that same manager understood that the idea of 'one size fits all' doesn't work and offered you a way of blending her insight with your experience so you could become the manager you were meant to be?

Real **management:**

- Makes sense of your experience by explaining why, when we do things by the book, they don't work.

- Is based on a common-sense understanding of human nature that takes your concerns seriously and starts from the assumption that what you're doing now makes sense for the situation you're in.

- Helps you turn your past experience into the key that unlocks your best ever management performance.

1

Confessions of an overworked manager

Towards a new way of managing in the *real* world

I'm tired of being overworked – are you?

I'm not a management guru. I'm an overworked manager who got sick of being overworked. I love my work so I give it 100 per cent . . . I push my team . . . we achieve things . . . I'm given more work . . . I give it 110 per cent . . . I push my team a bit harder . . . we achieve more things . . . I'm given more work . . . need I go on? Stress researchers say our automatic response to overload is to do what we were doing before only harder and for longer. Psychologists say insanity is doing the same things over and over and expecting different results. So, as they say in America, 'You do the math!'

There has to be a better way of working

Psychologists also say that if you want a different result, you have to do something different. Since I started my management career, I've seen (and been guilty of) the sorry way managers treat their staff (and vice versa), and I've become increasingly disillusioned with the established wisdom about managing people. I began to believe there had to be a better way.

> **Beliefs** are thoughts we use to guide our decisions and actions, although we tend to forget and see them as indisputable facts. With any action, a belief always comes first. We find evidence to support our beliefs in our experience. Once we've got a belief, we tend not to question it, unless an experience forces us to.

People shouldn't have to leave their brains at the door or become robots when they come into work. They shouldn't have to run ever harder just to stand still. In recent years, I've watched people go sick with stress and I've seen stress-management programmes being offered as the cure, all the time thinking that we must be in big trouble if we're settling for *managing* stress instead of removing it at source. I knew there had to be a way to remove the stress caused by the gap between who we are outside of work and who we have to be at work. There had to be a way of managing that isn't soul-destroying for everyone involved. I just didn't know what that way was. Then I met someone who changed the way I think about people; who motivated me to find a new way of managing; who influenced me to want to be a better manager; and who inspired me to take time out and write this series of books in the hope that I could do for others what he did for me.

There had to be a way of managing that isn't soul-destroying for everyone involved.

Getting out of the box of traditional management thinking

I started as a management trainee on a year's development programme, during which I became fascinated by the way people manage, and I've been a student of management as well as a manager ever since. I'm exaggerating (but, sadly, only slightly) when I say that by the time I decided there had to be a better way, I'd already read and tried everything ever published about management. Clearly, if I wanted new answers I had to look in new places. Not one to do things by halves, I've looked close to management, in neuroscience, psychology and psychotherapy to learn how our brains work, why we do the things we do, and how to deal with emotions and the effects of early conditioning on our behaviour. And I've looked far from management – everything from aikido to Zen Buddhism via horticulture and homoeopathy (well, if we aren't growing something as managers, we're curing it, right?). And yes, I confess, I've read almost everything the self-help movement has to offer, sifting the sensible from the senseless.

Looking for what makes sense

After years of being a task-focused manager working for organizations in 'initiative' mode, I can assure you I'm too sceptical about the 'next new idea' and the 'one size fits all' solution to have bought into any one set of beliefs. Instead, what I've done is collect and use the ideas that made sense of my experience. Small sentence, big idea, so let me say it again. I researched a wide range of subjects and whenever I got a feeling of 'that's obvious', I applied the idea to the way I manage and used my experience to figure out what worked.

> **Trial and error** is how we learn from experience – trying to do something, noticing what doesn't work, and changing our approach until we find what works. More often than not, we decide what works and doesn't work based on the feedback we get.

I want to make it easier for you than it was for me

It would be hypocritical for me to tell you I'm sceptical of people who sell you the 'one right way' and then try to do the same thing myself, so that's not what I'm doing. I'm sharing what I've learned to save you having to do all the research I did. But I can't do it all for you – we have to be in it together.

Equal partners or no deal

Ninety-five per cent of what we learn comes from experience, with only five per cent coming from books, training, etc., and they only work when they resonate with our own experience by triggering memories of earlier experiences.

> We have vast quantities of experience that we can't hold in our **conscious minds** so we store these experiences in our subconscious. The trouble with our **subconscious** is that it's sub (below) conscious (the level of our awareness) so we aren't conscious of (don't know) what's in there. We need triggers to surface it.

A good book is, in effect, telling you something you already know intuitively; you just haven't articulated it on a conscious level.

> **Intuition** is that feeling of knowing something, without knowing how you know it. It means you're using information from your subconscious mind that your conscious mind isn't aware of.

What I'm telling you will work only if you use my insight as a trigger for surfacing your experience and intuitive (subconscious) insight because, in the end, only your insight can improve your performance. It's 'equal partnership learning' – I provide the trigger, you provide the experience. I have no ambition to create clones of me. I want people to manage in a way that works for them – a way that suits their unique blend of insight and experience. What I *am* hoping for, though, is that you'll think what I'm saying is common sense.

> **Common sense** (a rarity in life) is when something is both logical (appealing to our conscious minds) and intuitive (appealing to our subconscious minds) and we get a 'that's obvious' feeling. When our conscious and subconscious minds are out of sync, we get an 'off' feeling – something isn't quite right, but we don't know why.

So, as you read this book, think about your experience and see if you get a 'that's obvious' feeling. If you do, then try my approach, learn from it, and adapt it to meet your needs. If you get an 'off' feeling, then challenge what I'm saying, come to your own insight, try that, learn from it, and adapt it to meet your needs.

Starting from where people are

The biggest mistake people make when trying to help move someone forward is to assume they're both starting from the same place – something that never happens in real life. I don't want to make that mistake with you, so throughout this book – in shaded boxes – I explain the concepts and beliefs that underpin my approach to management. In Appendix 1, there's also a broader look at where I'm coming from as a manager.

Let's keep it real here

If you're like most managers I know, you won't have time to read a heavyweight volume (even if I had time to write one), but you won't want to be fobbed off with one-minute answers that only work in books either. So what I've done (to give you the best of both worlds) is to put some powerful messages – that hopefully will resonate with your own experience and trigger your insight – into a quick but intense read. There's also a reminder of the key messages and some questions to think about at the end of each chapter.

Let me know what you think

I mean what I say about being equal partners, so if you want to share your experience and insight or ask questions about anything in the book, I'd really like to hear from you. You can email me at **JKSmartBooks@aol.com**. I take on a few telephone coaching clients each year so managers who are interested may email me as may trainers and development specialists who are interested in attending an 'equal partners learning programme' to be licensed to work with this material.

IN SHORT

- We can't keep doing what we've always been doing because it doesn't work and it stresses us out in the process.

- People who still tout the established management wisdom are 'flat earthers' who need to be challenged to develop an approach that works in the real world.

- I'm not telling you anything you don't already know: I'm only helping you to bring your insight to the surface where you can do something with it.

- Challenge everything I say, and take away only what makes sense of your experience.

2

The key to unlocking your best ever performance

Track back from your experience, then work forward from your beliefs

We already have everything we need to be effective

We just have preferences for, and are more skilled in, some things than others (a result of them being our preferences). Development, especially in people skills, isn't about teaching new skills as much as about unblocking existing ones. What blocks our development? Our beliefs, which govern how we use our characteristics. Lack of self-belief is the single biggest block to excellent performance. Once you get that sorted, everything else falls into place.

But our beliefs hinder us from using them

You may have excellent communication skills, but if you believe that talking never solved anything, then they're not likely to get much of an outing, so how will you ever know just how good they are? Have you ever thought, 'I wish I could do that but I'm not confident/bright/calm/etc. enough'? What are the component parts of the skill you wish you had? Do you use them in any other activity or part of your life?

And so do our judgements about ourselves

What's your biggest strength? Okay, in what kinds of situations does it really help you to perform well? Now identify at least one situation in which it hinders your performance. You may find this hard, but persevere, because I guarantee there will be at least one. If in doubt, ask a trusted colleague. Now, relabel the strength as a neutral word or phrase that would apply equally to both the helpful and hindering situations. When you've done that, try the same exercise again but this time for your biggest weakness and, suddenly, we don't have strengths and weaknesses any more; we have characteristics.

A **characteristic** is a piece of knowledge, an attitude, a behaviour, a skill, or any single input you bring to your performance. It is described neutrally to avoid implying strength or weakness. For example, I'm not lazy, I'm someone who doesn't like to waste energy. The same characteristic can be helpful or hindering depending on the context in which it is used.

The need to find and challenge our hindering beliefs

Are you happy with your results in all areas of your life? People are happy with their performance when the external world matches their inner reality and unhappy when it doesn't.

My definition of **sanity** is when the external world matches the picture of it that we have in our minds without us having to distort either what's out there or what's in our minds. It's when we see things as they are, not as we wish they were.

There are people who are happy or unhappy for healthy reasons (they see things as they really are and not as they'd like them to be). There are also people who are happy (but delusional) or unhappy (but victims) for unhealthy reasons (they distort what they see to conform to their inner reality).

Our **subconscious creates experiences** for us (from events) that reinforce what we believe about the world and the people in it, if necessary by distorting the picture so we see only what we want to see. But, while it does this to keep us feeling sane on a day-to-day basis (yes, even when all around us think we're delusional), it craftily creates negative experiences when it wants to push us into re-examining our beliefs. And if we don't re-examine our beliefs after a negative experience, it keeps recreating the same experience until we give in and do what it wants.

Effectiveness is when people are happy for healthy reasons. If you're not happy with the responses you're getting and the experiences you're creating, then you have three choices:

1. Carry on as you are, a victim in your own melodrama, blaming circumstances or other people and dragging the rest of us down with you.

2. Reframe the results so that you turn them into a positive experience that you can be happy about.

> **Reframing** is when we change our interpretation of an event, usually by challenging the beliefs that underpin our original interpretation. We do this by finding other ways of looking at it.

3. Assume what you got was what you wanted and track back to the beliefs that drove the behaviour. If you're okay with the beliefs, then go back to option 2. If you're not, then re-examine them and develop alternatives to change your behaviour and achieve different results.

We all know how to do option 1 but what about the rest? Easier said than done? Yes, if you associate change with behaviour change, but I'm talking about belief changes that take milliseconds to achieve and last forever and – and this is the big plus – a changed belief triggers a changed behaviour in ways that don't require mountains of will-power to sustain. Want to give it a try? Read on . . .

A changed belief triggers a changed behaviour without requiring mountains of willpower.

IN SHORT

- You've got everything you need already; it's only your beliefs that are holding you back.

- Stop being so hard on yourself: being judgemental and self-critical never helped anyone improve.

- Take the acid test: ask yourself if you're happy with the results that you are achieving.

◗ If you're not happy, don't just sit there; do something about it.

3

If it's as easy as the books make out, why are there so many books?

Resisting the temptation to want easy answers in a complex world

It's not my fault – it's the way I'm programmed

It's scientific fact, mother! Wanting easy answers doesn't make me lazy. Brains are hard-wired to lay down programmes in our subconscious so we can do things without thinking (on autopilot, if you like), leaving us with plenty of spare capacity to deal with the unexpected.

The brain develops **programmes** in our subconscious, based on our experiences. When it registers an unfamiliar event, it quickly (so quickly we don't know it's happening) looks for a suitable pre-existing programme (**pre-programme** for short) to interpret the event (like a computer matching fingerprints). When it registers a good enough match, it automatically triggers the response from the earlier experience.

Trainers call the pre-programmes that serve us well 'unconscious competence'.

At the bottom of the learning ladder is **unconscious incompetence** (when we don't know what we don't know), then **conscious incompetence** (when we realize we need to learn something), followed by **conscious competence** (when we're mastering a skill and still have to concentrate all the time we're doing it). This stage continues until we can do it without having to think (**unconscious competence**). Driving is the classic example.

So many choices – so little time

The trouble with being an overworked manager is that the only time I get a taste of the huge variety today's world has to offer is when I'm skimming the Sunday papers, and let's face it, who has time to do more than skim when there's so many sections? I used to like that line in Kipling's *If* about filling the unforgiving minute with 60 seconds' worth of distance run . . . until I had to live it! Ignoring the fact that some of today's time-saving devices don't actually do what they say on the tin (I'd mention email, but don't get me started on that or we'll be here all day), it's the ever increasing expectations of what we're meant to do with the time we save that get me. It's as though if we're not working flat out to improve the quality of our relationships, bodies, spirits and lifestyles – and don't forget careers – then we're somehow failing to make the most of everything that twenty-first-century life has to offer.

Is it any surprise that, as managers, we want one-minute answers to twenty-year problems? Who has time to spend with their staff these days, when the pressure to deliver more outputs with fewer resources is greater than ever? No wonder hypocrisy creeps in, as on a recent appraisal training course, where a group of management-level appraisees had no problem saying that for their own appraisal they wanted their manager to take as much time as it needed to do a good job, but that they were far too busy to do that for their team members.

The customer is king – so give them what they want

An IT manager asked me to approve a plan for recruiting IT officers for a number of local offices around the country. He wanted to run the selection process at HQ, with IT experts interviewing and then allocating successful candidates to local managers. He wanted the recruits to have high-quality IT skills, and he knew local managers weren't IT literate enough to ensure that. Something wasn't right with his proposal (my 'off' feeling), so I probed and discovered he feared local managers wouldn't have ownership of the national IT strategy if they'd had no say in the appointment of their IT officer. In the end, we recruited at local level with an IT person doing the shortlist (for quality control) and asking the technical questions, but with the local line manager making the final decision. The solution gave the IT manager everything he needed, which he wouldn't have got if I'd just given him what he wanted.

A lot of organizations buy into the 'customer is king' myth, and so must many management writers, otherwise quick-fix, autopilot, 'one-size-fits-all' solutions wouldn't be so prevalent on the management shelves of your local bookstore. Books that offer solutions that would insult your intelligence if you weren't so distracted by the demands of your job. Solutions that *do* insult your subconscious intelligence if only you had time to listen to it. And when you *do* look beyond the glib answers, what do you find? A complex world overcomplicated by impenetrable academics or the fashionable world of the latest management guru who thinks you can solve everything by applying an alarmingly alliterative acronym!

We need *real* answers for the way it is in the *real* world

Real managers run a mile from formulaic approaches that treat human beings as a constant when they're a variable. We know people make money by giving us what we want regardless of whether it's what we need, but in the *real* world what's important is what works, not what's quick. We need to find a way to meet our conscious need for easy answers with our subconscious need for a common-sense approach that works with the complexity of human nature.

IN SHORT

- We may be programmed to want easy answers, but we don't have to give in to temptation.

- We have so many choices about how to spend our time that it makes sense not to waste time getting our people management wrong.

- What we want isn't always what we need, so we need to think before we buy what's on offer.

▶ Yes, we *want* easy answers, but we *need* answers that work, so let's not settle for shabby compromise: let's get the best of both worlds.

PART 1

■ *real* management for the way it is ■

Understanding why delegation goes wrong so you can put it right

▶ Understanding the cause and effect relationships

As an overworked manager, I find it easy to get sucked into dealing with problems at symptom level rather than root cause. I get a buzz out of taking decisive action so I find it hard to slow down and make the effort to understand why something has gone wrong, even though I know the buzz won't last any longer than my solution!

▶ Taking a long hard look at the way we delegate

If you're anything like me, you'll be itching to get straight to the 'how to do it' part. But remember, that's where we went wrong in the past, so please bear with me because we can't put something right unless we understand why it went wrong in the first place. In a quick read, I don't have time to give you lots of examples plus my insights so I'm going to explore one big example in depth. I've used a composite of several real-life experiences so I can highlight the issues that undermine our approach to delegating.

4

Why don't I like to delegate?

Our fears always make sense – it's our beliefs and responses we need to worry about

The 'dim' approach to delegating

Delegating used to be something I only came across when my boss did it to me. I was the Do-It-Myself type (or 'dim' if you'll pardon the Hugh Grant style humour). My boss delegated (he liked a nap in the afternoon) badly and often but when I think how much I learned from doing his work, I could kick myself for the chances I've missed to develop my own team by delegating.

What's there to fear?

A while back, I was asked to design an appraisal system for managers in an organization that had never had one before. I told myself that no one in my team had ever designed one; conveniently ignoring the fact that I'd been an appraisal novice too at one time and things had worked out fine. If you delegate a task to someone else, there can only be one of four outcomes. They can produce something that is:

1. Worse than you would have produced yourself.

2. Equal to, and the same as, what you would have produced yourself.

3. Equal to, but different from, what you would have produced yourself.

4. Better than you would have produced yourself.

As a perfectionist, over-helping, control freak who thrives on being needed, all four outcomes are scary to me but, with appraisal, it was the first that stopped me delegating. Although there was no cynicism to overcome, there was no feedback or self-awareness culture either, so introducing appraisal was like doing the high jump from a standing start. I believed that if we were to succeed in changing the culture, the appraisal system had to be just right and that I was the only one who could do it.

Fear is nature's way of saying 'trouble ahead', so listen to it

The stakes were high so I acted on my fear and did it myself. My previous experience helped people believe that appraisal would be a good thing which encouraged them to make it work. And if that's all there were to report, it would be a happy ending, but there were two other unintended outcomes. First, I put so much personal time in that my other work suffered. And second, when I had to extend appraisal by designing a system for frontline staff (a much bigger task than I could accomplish alone), there was still no one else in the team who could do it.

Looking past the fear to the underlying belief that generates the response

I was convinced, by my success, that I was right to have done it myself and equally convinced, by the problems I'd created for the future, that I should have delegated it. A classic case of cognitive dissonance or what?

Cognitive dissonance happens when we try to hold two opposing thoughts at the same time. The mind can't cope with it, so works hard to get rid of the inconsistency (dissonance) in one of three ways:

1. By reducing the importance of the inconsistent beliefs.

2. By increasing the number of consistent beliefs to outweigh the dissonant ones.

3. By reinterpreting the inconsistent beliefs so they're no longer inconsistent.

I know a smoker who uses all three!

I wish I'd realized that beliefs are just thoughts we haven't questioned in a long time. My belief that the appraisal system had to be good to work withstands challenge but where did my belief – that I was the only person who could make it good enough – come from? And before you mock, tell me you've never succumbed to the old classic 'If you want a job doing properly, do it yourself'? Why, I bet you've got as much evidence to prove you're right as I

Beliefs are just thoughts we haven't questioned in a long time.

had with appraisal. Of course, given how our Reticular Activating System (RAS) works, we're bound to say that, aren't we?

> **Reticular Activating System (RAS)** is a brain function that makes us notice things that are significant to us but not notice things that aren't. We need it because there's so much information to process all the time that without it we couldn't function. But guess which bit of the brain decides what we need and don't need to see? That's right, the subconscious!

So, is it possible to be better at *every aspect of a task* than our staff? My first (ego-driven) thought was that I'm good at all aspects of appraisal development except one – form design. No spatial awareness, I'm afraid, so, why didn't I at least delegate the form design part of the appraisal project? On deeper reflection, I had to admit that completer-finishing, remembering to chase people, keeping records and doing routine tasks aren't really my thing either, so why didn't I delegate those too?

There's no such thing as 'seeing is believing' – quite the reverse in fact

Because my RAS wouldn't let me, that's why. If someone genuinely believes that 'if you want a job doing properly, you have to do it yourself', what will they see everywhere? Exactly . . . examples of people not doing the job as well as they can do it themselves. And what will they not see? Any evidence to make them question their belief. I'm embarrassed to confess that I now know I have two people on my team who design forms much better than I do but I didn't see it until I was delegating a boring (to me anyway) form design project. And as for completer-finishing . . .

IN SHORT

- **There will always be lost opportunities when you do it yourself instead of delegating.** What are you missing out on?

- **Our fears give us important information, so we need to listen to them.** What are your fears about delegating telling you?

- **It's our beliefs we need to worry about.** Is your RAS at work keeping you from seeing what's really there?

- **And our responses.** What's your typical response to the opportunity to delegate?

5

Why, when I delegate, don't I get what I want?

Funny how we don't really know what we want until we don't get it

Making your expectations clear

Having designed the appraisal system, I was ready to implement it for 3,000 managers. But first, I needed a training course. I'm not a professional trainer and I wasn't going to repeat my form design mistake, so I delegated it.

I spent a good deal of time with David, sharing my vision for appraisal as being about the appraiser and appraisee coming together to get a better understanding of the appraisee's performance, so the right development could be identified and performance improved. To me, the forms were just a record of the discussion. I gave him copies of the forms, policy, and notes for guidance and answered all his questions. At the end of the briefing process, I was confident that he understood my objectives and, with his training expertise, would be able to convert them into a great course.

Or not, as the case may be

Before he got too far into his task, David gave me his course outline to check I was happy with the direction he was taking. It started with a group exercise on the benefits of appraisal, then took people through the process. The course didn't overtly focus on the forms but they were always brought in at the point at which each session ended, so suffered from the recency effect.

> The **primacy and recency effect** describes the fact when we're given a long list of things to memorize, we're more likely to remember the first (primacy) and last (recency) thing on the list.

I could guess from the course structure that he'd used the process and forms as his frame of reference for developing the course.

> A **frame of reference** is just a collection of beliefs that we use to make sense of something we're doing or an event we're interpreting. It's a bit like putting a coloured lens over our eyes and looking through that.

I knew as soon as I saw David's course outline that it wasn't what I wanted. I'm ashamed to admit that just as suddenly and just as clearly, I knew exactly what I *did* want. I just didn't know how I knew it. I knew that no matter how much we said that appraisal isn't a form-filling exercise, if our behaviour on the course gave a strong counter-message, then that's the message people would take away. We needed consistency between our words and our deeds and, for that, we needed a radical new approach to training.

> When we're listening, our conscious pick up the words and the more obvious behaviour and our subconscious picks up the rest. Because **our subconscious notices everything** and because it's stronger than our conscious, we tend to form our judgements from the way people behave, not from what they say. **Our subconscious is designed to spot inconsistencies,** which it tells us about through our intuition. Because all this happens below our level of consciousness, we often just get a feeling that we don't trust someone. But if we analyzed it, we'd find we've picked up an inconsistency between their words and deeds.

I wanted to teach appraisal with a small 'a' – the kind we do everyday when we need to interpret an event. I wanted to use the course to show people the problems we encounter when we appraise people on an everyday basis and show them how to do it better when we have someone's career in our hands.

We can only ask for what we are conscious of wanting

Let me say it again. I knew *as soon as I saw it* that it wasn't what I wanted and, *just as suddenly,* I knew what I did want. Do you see what I'm saying? For my reaction to have been that quick and that sure, I must have known all along exactly what I wanted. So why didn't I tell David at the beginning? Because I didn't know it consciously, I only knew it subconsciously and it took David not meeting my subconscious expectations for me to become conscious of them.

> **Subconscious expectations** are simply pre-programmes that create beliefs about what to expect in certain situations or with certain people.

The trouble with subconscious expectations is that – well – they're subconscious!

And a fat lot of good they'll do for the person you are delegating to if that's where they stay. You can get to your subconscious expectations by asking what feels 'off' to you. In this case, it was David taking a 'professional trainer' approach to developing the course that made me realize I expected courses for managers to be designed from a managerial perspective (for customer empathy). David was a professional trainer, so it was hardly his fault that he had that perspective. I should have combined my managerial perspective with his trainer perspective so we could get the best of both worlds. Ah, the joys of hindsight.

IN SHORT

- **We can only brief people on what's in our conscious minds at the time.** When did you last have an experience like mine with David and what did you learn from it about your subconscious expectations?

- **We need to find easier ways of surfacing what's in our subconscious.** Apart from failure to meet them, what else works for you as a trigger to bring your subconscious expectations to the surface?

▶ **We get an 'off' feeling when something we're seeing or hearing doesn't add up to our conscious and subconscious minds**. When did you last get an 'off' feeling about someone and what was it telling you?

6

Why, no matter how well I brief my staff, does it still go wrong?

It's always a mistake to assume you're starting with a clean sheet

The world's longest briefing session

After my false start with David, I took a belt and braces approach. I invited the external trainers we'd hired to deliver the course to join us on a two-day course development event. That way, everyone would be singing from the same hymn sheet – and it would be my hymn sheet (have I mentioned my control freak tendencies?). I explained my Eureka moment about an appraisal-with-a-small-'a'-course and we spent the next two days developing ideas. Everyone said it was a great success and that we'd found the key to unlocking people's prejudices in a way that didn't make them feel bad about having them in the first place. We'd developed exercises that just needed a bit more work and putting together in a sensible order. After that, all David had to do was write the formal 'chalk and talk' bits and the handouts and we were done.

But obviously not quite long enough

A couple of weeks later, David came back to me with a full draft course – input, handouts, exercises, the whole works. I can't get a feel for how a course will work just by reading the script, so we did a 'walkthrough'.

A **'walkthrough'** is rehearsing an event or process in your head by describing in detail what's happening from start to finish. A walkthrough feels like you're doing a running radio commentary on a fantasy football match, describing the action both on and off the ball. One person describes what's happening and the others ask questions to make sure no details get missed. You have to remember to keep asking questions of the 'where's the ref at this point?' kind, so you are sure nothing and no one gets missed. It sounds weird but it's great for anticipating potential problems.

The 'walkthrough' was an eye-opener. I noticed things that suggested that although David had moved away from his trainer perspective, he was still working within a process frame of reference. He was still calling the course after the name of the appraisal system, instead of giving it a more generic title like 'appraising people'. And there were oft-repeated references to having a proper look at the forms in the last session. There was something else that felt 'off' too. Although the hard-sell opening exercise had gone, hearing him do the 'walkthrough', I still got a sense of defensiveness about the appraisal system which gave a strong message that we had something to defend. We didn't – our system was open, honest, transparent and fair to all parties.

You're not the only one with subconscious expectations

I asked David a lot of questions that afternoon about his experience of appraisal.

> **Experience = event + interpretation**
> Very little of what we call our experience is made up of things that happen to us (events). Most of it is about how we interpret (make sense of) those events.

The appraisal system in his last organization had been pay related with rating scales and was seen by staff as threatening. There had been a lot of cynicism directed at David who had delivered the appraisal training. He'd had a hard time justifying the system and dealing with the cynicism. Although on a conscious level he didn't think our system would generate the same response, he had a subconscious expectation that it would. Once we'd surfaced it, we identified his underlying beliefs and challenged them.

Don't just listen to your own fears

We listened to his fears and amended the course to explain why we didn't have ratings scales or links to pay. But we did it in a matter-of-fact way so it didn't look like we were expecting to defend ourselves against negative reactions. David's fear was valid (even people with no personal experience of appraisal will have heard horror stories from friends) but he'd focused on only one of his beliefs about appraisal – that it would be seen as a threat. He needed to develop a response to his fears that also accommodated his belief that appraisal, done properly, was a very positive thing.

Despite my expectation that David would be a bit fed up by now with all the chopping and changing, he was fine about reworking the course. He told me later that it meant a lot to him that I'd taken his fears seriously even though, on the face of it, they weren't rational. For my part, I felt the amendments we'd included as a result of listening to his fear had made the course better.

IN SHORT

▶ **You're not the only one with subconscious expectations.** When were you last surprised by something a team member clearly expected that would never have occurred to you?

▶ **Our experience of an event often bears little resemblance to the experience of the other people involved.** How does your last experience of delegating compare to the way your team member experienced it?

▶ **We need to listen to our team members' fears as well as our own.** What kinds of things do your team members worry about and what do you do about them?

7

Why, even when I get exactly what I asked for, am I still disappointed?

In *real* life we never just implement our first idea, we adjust as we go

Sticking to the brief no matter what the cost

David came back with the course he'd redesigned and it was now completely true to the work we'd done with the external trainers – an excellent piece of work. So why was I disappointed? Because, when I read the script, there just didn't seem to be a natural flow from one session to the next. It reminded me of that sketch where Eric Morecambe says he's playing all the right notes but not necessarily in the right order!

I sometimes get **'flow' problems** when I'm reading draft reports and have a simple technique for putting things right. I cover up everything except the first paragraph which I read as if I'm new to the subject. Then I pause and see what questions come to me. Then I uncover the next paragraph to see if it ▶

either answers them or gives a cross-reference to the answer.
If it doesn't do either, I find the answer and either move it so it
flows or add a cross-reference. Then I repeat the process for
each paragraph in the rest of the report. Once you get the
knack, it doesn't take very long and it can really transform an
uninspiring or unpersuasive read.

The flow technique had left me with unanswered questions,
so I knew there must be gaps in the course that needed to be
filled. We'd have to abandon a couple of the exercises I'd
developed to make room, but that wasn't a problem. The
problem was that I was pretty sure that if I asked David to
make more changes, he'd lose his cool. He'd been pretty
patient with me so far but probably felt he'd been back to the
drawing board enough times already. Besides, it was fine as it
was – nothing wrong with it. It was just that I thought we
could make it better.

I thought discretion would be the better part of valour so I
decided to see if I could get David to see the problems for himself so that it would be him initiating the changes, not me. I'm
a big fan of using real work as a basis for staff development so
I decided to show him how to do my flow technique. It worked
well and he was quick to see what I'd seen. We talked about
how we might make the changes and what difference it would
make to the impact of the learning points. David went away,
made the changes and when he ran the pilot he was delighted
with how it had gone.

Doing a review for learning

David had been so busy making the last-minute changes then running the pilot course that we hadn't had time for our usual review for learning session.

I regularly do reviews for learning with my team – sometimes one to one and sometimes with a whole project group, depending on the issue. We prepare by considering the following questions first on our own and then together.

- What went well and less well? What did I do to contribute to the outcome? What do I know now that I didn't know before?
- What have I learned about behaviour (about myself, the way other people behave, etc.)? What insight have I gained about dealing with this kind of experience in the future?
- To enable me to use what I have learned, what, if anything, do I need to change about the way I think or the way I behave? Are there any old ideas or behaviours I need to unlearn first?
- How, where and when can I use this insight to improve my performance?

When we finally did the review, I learned David simply hadn't thought about changing things. He'd seen his job as delivering the brief according to the specification we'd produced in the development workshop.

What, if anything, do I need to change about the way I think or the way I behave?

Giving people permission to make the task their own

David had been given a brief by his boss. His commitment to delivering that overrode his natural tendency to adjust things on the basis of the insight he'd gained through actually doing the task. He clearly believed that as he was doing the task for me, I should be the one to make any adjustments. The only problem with that was that I wasn't doing the task, so I hadn't gained any insight about what changes needed to be made. I was relying on his insight which he was ignoring! What was strange was that, after we'd had that discussion, David was okay with making adjustments based on his experience of doing the task. It was as if he'd only needed my permission.

IN SHORT

▶ **We never stick to our own brief (we adjust as we go) but our team members often don't feel they can do likewise.** Have you had an experience like mine with David?

▶ **With clear ground rules on referring back, we need to give our staff permission to work with the insight they gain from doing the task.** How would it feel to allow the brief to be the starting point not the finishing point?

▶ **When you delegate a task, you lose the experience gained from doing it yourself, so you need regular reviews for learning.** How often do you sit down with your team members and find out what they are learning from their experience?

8

Why do things go wrong if I'm not checking up on them all the time?

Delegating the task but not the responsibility for managing the task

Someone is managing the process

We had a great course. Now all we had to do was deliver it to 3,000 managers and make sure they actually got appraised shortly after they'd been trained. David asked senior managers in each department to submit a plan with dates against the names of all their managers showing – 'do not train this manager before this date or after this date', together with the date on which the appraisal would take place. I delegated the implementation management to David just before I went off on my summer holiday. By the time I got back he had a system in place for getting monthly reports from each department on numbers trained and appraised. Everything seemed to be going well so I turned my attention to other things. I looked at the figures every month but, if I'm honest, it was a cursory glance. Well . . . David had it covered.

Or maybe not

I was having my usual quick look at the fourth monthly report. The statistics told me a lot more people had been trained than had been appraised and something told me to dig a bit. It wasn't my conscious, because logic said the statistics were a reflection of the normal time lag between training and appraisal, so it must have been my subconscious telling me it had expected the figures to look different . . . maybe it had been taking more notice of the previous reports than I had! The problem was, I couldn't tell whether there was a real problem just from looking at the statistics. After all, they only summarized what was actually happening, not what was supposed to be happening, so there was nothing to compare the figures to. And because the statistics being collected weren't in the same format as those in the plans, we couldn't solve it just by getting the plans out.

I've learned the hard way to listen to my intuition, so I got the team to find out whether there was indeed a problem (it turned out to be a combination of people getting ahead of the plan with the training and behind the plan with the appraisal) and how far off plan each department was. We got some departments back on track and others to adjust their plans where they'd overestimated their capability. It was good that we acted

I've learned the hard way to listen to my intuition.

when we did, as we were starting to get complaints from appraisees who had been trained and were keen to be appraised. The long delays they were facing in being appraised meant we were in danger of losing the goodwill needed to make the system work.

You can't manage if you can't compare what is happening with what should be

We were due to launch another major programme in a couple of months so we needed to learn everything we could from this problem. In our review for learning, it became clear that though everyone had been beavering away doing their tasks, they'd been administering and coordinating the process, rather than managing it. As each course took place, they'd been collecting information on who was attending and they'd also been collecting the statistics from the departments. However, they were only using them once a month to write the reports, not on a daily basis to make sure everything was happening as it should.

> When people **administer** a process they are in essence just processing their bits of it. And **coordinating** is just about ensuring other people process their bits. **Managing** is what people are doing when they're making sure that what is supposed to be happening *is* happening and doing something about it, if it's not.

David and his team were doing the task but not managing it – they thought that was *my* job. And, in so far as it's possible to manage something on the basis of historical reports, I was following up on anything that didn't look right. But that's not real management. My team were getting information every day which should have been generating management interventions, instead of which, it was generating reports.

You need the right feedback to make the right adjustments

A pilot friend told me that planes are almost never flying on course. During the flight, pilots (or the plane when it's on autopilot) make lots of little corrections based on feedback from the instruments.

Feedback is the signs we pick up about reactions to what we're doing. It's not just the formal feedback you get when your boss reviews your work, it's all the little signals we don't necessarily notice consciously but that our subconscious picks up and uses to adjust our thinking, behaviour and actions. We get feedback all the time whether we think we do or not. Without feedback, we'd never know how to adjust course to achieve our intentions.

But what if you haven't got any instruments or if the instruments you have don't tell you what you need to know to adjust your course? It's the same with people.

IN SHORT

▶ **We need to delegate the responsibility for managing the task as well as for doing it.** Who managed the last task you delegated?

▶ **Management is taking action to make sure that what is happening is what should be happening.** How much do you really manage?

◗ **People need regular feedback of the right kind to manage tasks effectively**. What makes you notice things that indicate you're not on the right track?

9

Why, even when I do everything right, does it still go wrong?

Because we're human beings, not robots – thank goodness!

What I learned from my delegation experience

I learned that if I'd been a better delegator, I'd have involved David from the beginning, improved the expertise within the team, and got a better result. And if I'd surfaced our assumptions earlier, we'd have saved a lot of time and rework. Of course, if I'd treated David like an adult not a child, he'd have felt able to apply his own insight to the task and he'd have managed the task for himself instead of expecting me to mother him through it.

Asking the tough questions

If we don't get the results we want, we may need to accept that, no matter how much we know logically (consciously) that we need to delegate more, our subconscious wants something else more. And whatever it is, our subconscious will sabotage our efforts until we resolve the dissonance. If your delegation attempts haven't worked as you would have liked, it may be because you fell into some of the same traps I did. But before you start changing your approach, it's worth checking to see if you really do want to delegate – by asking yourself . . .

What do I gain when delegation goes wrong?

Does having to step in and save the day make you feel indispensable? Are you more self-confident when there's clear water between what you and your staff can do? Does doing it yourself keep you so busy in your comfort zone that you don't have to face the rigours of stretching yourself? I answered yes to all these questions. Making the admission worth the effort means not self-judging but accepting that human beings are complex. We do the best we can at the time to respond to our needs using the options we think we have at our disposal. It doesn't make us bad people, it just makes us human. But what if we don't use what we've learned to move ourselves forward? Well, maybe that's when we should be getting the birch twigs out!

You already have everything you need to be a great delegator

Events happen, we interpret them which makes them an experience, then we store them in our subconscious. So why aren't we already effective? The reasons may be:

■ The way we interpreted the event – which caused us to believe something that isn't realistic. Did we miss something by only looking at it one way?

- We're only working with our conscious mind (our logic) – so we're not listening to our subconscious mind (our intuition) and we're not accessing our experience.

- We're only working with our subconscious – operating on autopilot and not using our conscious mind to check that what we're doing is logical. We're acting like children not adults.

The only way to be effective is to have your logic and intuition in balance . . . it's only common sense, after all.

Use this book to trigger your subconscious knowledge and insight

If people learn from experience, what's the point of reading a book? No point at all, if you don't make it into an experience. Remember:

Event + Interpretation = Experience

So if you just read the book, you've had an event and not an experience and you won't learn anything from it. A good book will do three things:

- It will make you think, interpret and maybe challenge some of your beliefs and, in doing so, will become an 'experience' in its own right.

- It will bring to the surface things you already know on a subconscious level from your experience of life so you can look more closely at them.

- It will expose you to someone else's experience so you can learn from that as you would from your own experience, only faster.

But it won't work if you read it on autopilot

I hope as you read the rest of the book, you will pause every time something I say triggers either of the following responses:

■ If you want to say 'that's obvious', then stop and ask yourself 'Am I acting on what I know?' and 'Would other people be able to tell that's what I believe from the way I behave?'

■ If you get an 'off' feeling, stop and work out what's making you feel like that. You don't have to agree with everything I say, you just have to find what makes sense to you.

IN SHORT

▶ **We do what makes sense to us so suspend self-judgement and look for your logic.** What do you have to gain when your delegation attempts go wrong?

▶ **If we're not as effective as we'd like to be, we need to reinterpret our experiences.** Looking back to your last experience of delegation, what might a neutral observer say you'd missed?

▶ **A good book will trigger things your subconscious knows already.** What has made sense to you so far?

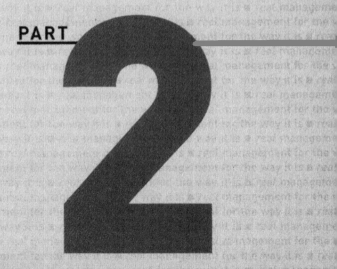

PART

2

■ *real* management for the way it is ■

Getting delegation right in the *real* world

▶ **Being too process-orientated gets us into more trouble than we know**

If you're anything like me, you've skipped straight to this page because it explains the delegation process from first thoughts to final review for learning. Never mind telling me why it goes wrong, I hear you mutter, just tell me how to do it right. I wish I could but, sadly:

■ Learning is about trial and error and the more you can learn from my trials and errors (in Part 1) the less time you need to waste doing your own.

■ When it comes to getting results in the real world, you can't pin your faith on the kind of task-orientated processes that operate in most organizations. Why not? Because human beings have a habit of putting spanners in the works of even the best laid processes.

Process is important, I grant you (there's really no other way to get from start to finish in anything we do) but a process that's been designed without a proper understanding of what *can* go wrong, *will* go wrong.

How many times have you felt that you were serving a process that should be there to serve you? On my good days, I see process as a necessary evil and on my bad days it's the enemy that makes me manage like a robot. And speaking of enemies, I like the martial arts idea of deflecting your opponent's strength against itself, so I design inclusive processes that take account of all the things that normal processes leave out, things that make me more people-orientated.

▶ It's not my process that matters – it's yours

Most management writers will tell you 'follow this process and you'll be fine'. I only wish it was true. But the truth is, no one but you can know what it's like in your world, so no one but you can design a delegation process that works for you. What I can do is describe seven generic steps that will identify all the things you need to think about when you're designing your own delegation process. So, as you read through each step, remember the insights you got from reading Part 1 and think about how you can use the process to help you address those issues.

10

How do you make sure your delegation process will work?

Understanding the variables so you can manage the dynamic

It's not just people who have characteristics – tasks do too

Among other things, tasks can be easy or hard, big or small, complex or routine, controversial or consensual, new or old, one-off or regular, stand-alone or part of a larger task, in the day job or an add-on, involving just you or other people, within your control or needing someone else's agreement. What are the characteristics of a task you're thinking of delegating?

The characteristics of a task affect how you do it. What's the difference between the way you approach an easy task and a hard task? Easy first and hard last? Now, ask yourself what effect that approach has on the task? I don't give myself enough time to do a good job on the very tasks that need most time (oh dear). Now try asking the same questions about each of the characteristics of the task you're thinking of delegating and see how it's affected by the way you react.

What are the outputs and outcomes of the task you're thinking of delegating?

> We produce **outputs** (things) to achieve **outcomes** (results). The trouble is, we're often so focused on the outputs that we lose sight of the outcomes, yet we exist to deliver outcomes not outputs. There are always more outcomes than you think. For example, if you're working with partners to develop a new product/service, there'll be an outcome about the quality of your relationship and, if you don't pay attention, it might not be an outcome you want.

Which are the most important outcomes for this task? How do they affect the outputs you need to achieve? I had a colleague who believed a good relationship with the unions was more important than getting a particular output. Without judging his belief as good or bad, think about how his need for a positive relationship outcome might affect his approach to doing the task.

The task doesn't do itself – the performer affects the dynamic

We've already seen one way in which the performer affects the performance by considering the effect our approach to the task has on the dynamic. Another thing is our characteristics. I'm better at written communication than spoken, so I often rely on reports to persuade people. What characteristics do you rely on in doing the task and how do they affect the way you do it?

Your operating context has a huge effect on the dynamic

Operating context includes anything or anyone in your organizational or external environment that affects performance of the task. Primarily that means people (customers, suppliers, colleagues, staff and stakeholders), your organizational culture and the external environment in which your organization works.

Among other things, an organization's culture can be entrepreneurial or bureaucratic, procedure driven or people driven, controlling or empowering, 'can-do' or 'can't-do', service orientated or product orientated. How would you describe your organization's culture and how **Where do you fit into the** does it affect the task? I had a job **organization?** once where, despite being only two steps down from the Chief Executive, I couldn't sign my own memos! Where do you fit into the organization? How does your position affect the way you do the task? Do you have the power you need to get the results?

Apart from you, who has a stake in the task?

I divide **stakeholders** into **interest and impact groups**. Impact groups can prevent you achieving the outcomes. Interest groups will be affected by the outcome but can't prevent you achieving the outcomes. You can't ignore the needs of either group, but the distinction helps when you're managing a conflict of interests.

Each group or individual stakeholder will have an agenda that will affect the task. What do your stakeholders want and what difference do they make to the way you approach the task?

Your organization doesn't exist in a vacuum, so how does the world outside affect how you do the task? And how does your job as a whole affect the task? How does this task stack up against everything else you have to do? Is it crucial to your success?

The variables don't just affect the task – they affect each other

I've looked at the different variables one at a time because it's easier; but they don't operate in isolation, all having a separate linear effect on the task. They affect one another (for example, stakeholders will be involved in the task to different degrees in different types of organizations) which is what makes the dynamic so . . . dynamic! And of course, if you alter one of the variables you alter the whole dynamic.

A different performer, a different set of characteristics

We've already established that it's only natural for us to play to our strengths. Everyone does it – including the team member you're thinking of delegating to. What strengths does that team member have? Are they the same or different to yours? How might their reliance on their strengths affect the way they do the task? What difference might it make compared to how you do the task?

And a different perspective – on the task

When you were establishing the characteristics of the task, did you think it was easy or hard? If the task is one you do regularly and are comfortable with, I imagine you thought it was easy. If the task is new to your team member, are they more likely to think it's hard? Of course, even if they agree with you about the characteristics of the task, they may have a different approach to those same characteristics. I have a colleague who actually likes to do the hard things first! How might your team member be different to you in the way they view the task's characteristics? And what about the way they view the outputs and outcomes? No matter how much you stress the important ones, your team member's subconscious will surely affect their approach. What do you think your team member would think are the most important outcomes in the task? Are they different from the ones you chose?

And on the operating context

It goes without saying that your team member doesn't have the same position (or power) in the organization as you do. They won't always be able to make the same things happen that you can and the limitations on their power will affect how they approach the task. Are there any differences in the way you'd have to approach the task if you were at the same level in the organization as your team member?

And would they describe the characteristics of the organizational culture in the same way as you? If you thought your organization was a 'can-do' culture because that was your experience but your team member experienced it as a 'can't-do' culture, what difference might that make to the way they do the task compared to you? Might they want to minimize the risks, get more second opinions, push decisions up the line?

What kind of relationship does your team member have with the various stakeholders for this task? How is it different from your relationship with them? You know how much easier it is to make things happen when you have a good relationship with someone than it is when you're cold-calling them.

And don't forget to think about where the task stands in relation to your team member's job as a whole. If they are doing something that's part of your job, no matter how routine a task you thought it was, they're bound to see it as more important, because they're more exposed.

And on the new variable – you!

When you delegate you become part of the dynamic to your team member so their perspective of you affects the way they approach the task. What does your team member think of you? What messages have you given them over the years through your behaviour? Will they see delegating as a chance to develop their performance or as you offloading the boring bits of your job?

What does your team member think of you?

It's all just a matter of perspective

And if you want to prove it, just ask your team member to answer all the questions I asked you about the task you are thinking of delegating and see how many of your answers match up.

> Our **perspective** is what we see from the position we are looking from. Anyone in a different position from you (a stakeholder, customer, team member, your boss) is bound to see things differently. As our actions are based on our interpretation of what we see and hear, a different perspective may lead to a different interpretation and so to different action.

Everyone's perspective shifts over time

Everything we see and hear has the potential to shift our perspective and we are constantly shifting and fine-tuning it over time on the basis of our experience. And our perspective on a task will be changed by our experience of doing it, which can make us want to change our approach to the task in the middle of doing it. How many tasks have you viewed as easy until your boss moved the goalposts?

Everything we see and hear has the potential to shift our perspective.

IN SHORT

▶ **The task, the performer and the operating context all affect the way a task is done.** How might your delegation process work differently if you analyzed the variables before you delegated?

- **Everyone brings something different to the task.** What do you bring to the task that is unique to you and what does your team member bring that's different to you?

- **Nothing stays the same, perspectives shift over time.** If you'd known at the start of the task what you knew at the end, what might you have done differently?

11

How do you avoid the 'task focus' trap and build your process around the 'human element'?

Understanding yourself and the person you're delegating to

You are a simultaneously complex and simple human being

You're the sum total of all your thoughts, choices, characteristics, actions, results and experience. You're all the judgements of others that you now use to judge yourself. You're the person you're trying to be and the person you're trying not to be. You're an amazing concoction of values, principles, beliefs, pre-programmes, habits, tendencies, needs, drivers, coping strategies, defences, intentions, characters and the buttons other people push. And you're also the detached observer of yourself – the part that smiles at your eccentricities, that knows you're more than the sum of your parts. Finally, and

> **You're the person you're trying to be and the person you're trying not to be.**

most importantly, you're the Director – the one who pulls together your cast of characters to create your performance.

I guess even the most sceptical of us would accept that different relationships and different situations bring out **different 'sides' to our character**. I like to think of the 'sides' of my character as characters in their own right because it helps me keep a sense of humour when one of them does something daft. Each of your cast of characters represents a need that won't go away just because you ignore it and is often associated with a cluster of characteristics you don't use any other time.

Let's give your detached observer a chance to look at a few complexities you bring to your delegation performance.

You are your beliefs – the ones that shape your behaviour

I used to believe delegation took a lot more time than doing it myself and gave me a poorer quality product to boot and my experience always confirmed the rightness of my belief. Now I believe that the most important task I do at work is manage, develop and empower my team and that delegation is a brilliant tool for doing all three. Funny thing is, my experience still confirms the rightness of my belief even though my belief has changed. What must you believe about delegation to have got the result you did? Now, imagine you had the opposite belief? What might you do differently?

You are your drivers – the ones that guide your choices

Everything we do is designed by our conscious or subconscious to meet one need or another – even the apparently unselfish things. Understanding which needs come into play when you delegate means you can accommodate them in your delegation system.

Like most things to do with human nature, our **needs** are simultaneously complex and simple. Simple because we only have two core needs – avoid pain and get pleasure (or, as we get older and more sophisticated, to avoid negative consequences and seek positive consequences). Complex because our beliefs about what causes pain and pleasure are unique to us.

I accommodate my need to control by insisting team members do excellent task management. Find your needs:

- Identify your delegation fears. It was fear of losing control that made me realize there's no point having a delegation system that pretends I'm laid back!

- Think about what made you feel 'off' during your worst ever delegation experience. It's often a sign of a need not being met. I feel edgy if my team member doesn't keep me informed often enough, so there's no point my having a delegation system that gives the task away and never sees it again.

You are your choices – the ones you make to achieve your intentions

When we react without first pausing to reflect, it's our sub-conscious working without listening to our conscious (logic). Look at your worst delegation experience again and identify the point at which things started to go bad. What were you reacting to? What did you achieve with your choice? Now, mentally step back into that moment and ask yourself the following questions:

- What other options did I have for responding in that moment of choice?
- What would the consequences of each option have been?
- Which option would have given me the best result?

You are your characteristics – the ones you acknowledge *and* the ones you don't

Sometimes we limit our potential by identifying too closely with a characteristic we admire in ourselves to compensate for the existence of its polar opposite which we deny. My biggest strength is creativity. It helps me solve delegation problems but it hinders me because it stops people solving their own problems. The opposite of creating is maintaining, a characteristic I disown because it doesn't fit my image of myself as an artiste! Yet, I maintain my friendships so I know I must have it and maybe if I owned it I'd be able to sustain some of the results of my creativity a bit more. What's your biggest strength in delegating? How does it help your delegation and how does it hinder it? What's its polar opposite and what difference might it make to your delegating if you accepted you had that characteristic too?

Above all, you are your Director – who pulls the whole performance together

If it all seems too complex even to think about, let me cheer you up by reminding you that we're the superior species. We're not unconscious creatures, programmed just to follow our instinct – well not *my* readers anyway. We have consciousness and the ability to reason. Sooner or later, your Director looks at your results and asks 'Am I happy with this performance?' If the answer is 'yes, fine' then you and your complexities get to carry on as before. And if it's 'no', your Director evokes the first rule of directing – 'If you want a different result do something different'. See, it's not so complex after all. Just change one thing at a time until your Director says that's a wrap!

We're not unconscious creatures, programmed just to follow our instinct.

Managing people goes wrong when we think we already know the answer

Remember as a child, asking 100 questions a minute? The more we learn, the more we think we know and the fewer questions we ask. So, if we think we already know why someone has done something, we don't ask. And that's the problem in a nutshell. We treat assumptions like facts. I have a friend who rings me once a week when I'm in her good books and once a month when I'm in her bad books. So, when she hasn't rung for a couple of weeks, I know I'm in her bad books, right? Wrong. There could be a dozen different reasons why she hasn't called. I'm just making an assumption based on previous experience. And that's what gets us into trouble when we're analyzing people's behaviour.

Get into the right frame of mind to understand your team member

It's not easy being a detached observer when you're watching and listening to one of your team doing a task whose outcome affects you. Delegation is a different dynamic with each team member, so you need to know what makes them tick. If you're not naturally interested in people as people, just see it as a way of making your job easier.

Start with what you see and hear

Start observing their actions and reactions. Listen to when they offer opinions and ask why they think what they do and you'll soon get to their beliefs and fears. Here are a few tips to get you started:

- Use your imagination – try to imagine being the person you are observing so you can see how the world looks from their frame of reference.

I prefer **imagination** to **empathy** because empathy is so easy to get wrong. Too often people think empathy is about what we'd do if we were in someone else's situation. But we get it wrong because we take our own frame of reference with us whereas, if we actually *were* in their situation, we'd be looking from a different perspective so we'd do something different. Getting this wrong is often what stops us understanding people. For example, it's hard, from our perspective, to understand why someone would stay in an abusive relationship, but the person in the abusive relationship has a different perspective so their experience makes a different sense to them

- Look and listen between the lines – for implicit meanings as well as explicit ones and how what they're saying reveals their beliefs.

- Notice what's missing – what's *not* being said or done can tell you as much about a person as what *is* said and done. Are they holding something back?

Use your 'detached observer' to find their logic

Everyone has their own logic.

> My definition of **logic** is rational cause and effect. If you work backwards from the effects people achieve and ask yourself 'Why would someone want to do that?' you will find the belief that caused them to produce that effect – that's their logic.

Think about what you're seeing and hearing and try to identify what effect your team member is having on the person they are interacting with or the task they are doing. Now, assume for the sake of the analysis that they're trying to achieve that effect (consciously or subconsciously) and think about why anyone might want to achieve that effect.

Don't jump to conclusions

Brainstorm as many possible reasons for their behaviour as you can. Then, think about which reason makes most sense in the context of what else you know about the person. Once you've got your preferred reason, check to see if you're right. The easiest way to do this is to ask. I've found that if you explain to your team member what you've observed, then say you're just guessing and ask them whether they agree or disagree, you'll find they open up a lot more, partly because psychologically, they already know you're not judging them and partly because they'll feel you've been paying attention to them and that in itself will help them feel good.

Remember, people wear masks

A word of warning – we've all got a greater or lesser capacity to be in denial about ourselves so watch to see how your team member reacts to people giving them back what they give out. I remember a colleague who was blunt and in-your-face with everyone, often to the point of rudeness. Yet when I once saw someone do the same to her, she broke down and cried. It turned out that she had completely disowned her sensitive streak and her tough behaviour was only a mask.

> A **mask** is something we pretend we are, to cover something we are pretending we aren't. I have an arrogant streak I don't much like so I wear the mask of openness about things I'm not good at. It has a positive effect on others (they become open too) so I think of my mask as the positive side of my arrogant streak.

And what are you looking and listening for?

You don't need to know other people as well as you know yourself, but there are three things you need to know about each team member:

- Their characteristics – you especially need to know the situations in which they help and hinder.

- Their drivers – because if their work meets their needs, they'll be self-motivated.

- Their beliefs – because that's the only level at which you can influence their results in a sustainable way.

IN SHORT

▶ **You bring all your human complexity to the pursuit of your simple need to avoid pain and find pleasure.** What brings on the pains when you think about delegating and what would it take to make delegating a pleasurable experience?

▶ **You can ignore the bits you don't like or choose to live in the real world.** What difference could you make to your performance as a delegator if you accepted all of who you are and not just the bits you liked?

▶ **We make all sorts of assumptions but only rarely test them out.** When was the last time you discovered you'd been working on a false assumption?

▶ **Don't stay on the surface, look and listen between the lines.** When was the last time you felt that there was more to what you were hearing than what was being said?

▶ **Suspend your judgement and look for their logic.** When was the last time one of your team did something daft? Forget how they actually justified themselves, what was their real logic?

12

How do you ensure the responsibilities are properly allocated?

Shifting from a parent/child to an adult/adult relationship

If you want a different response, do something different

It happens to all of us. We do something for someone a few times, just to be helpful you know, but before we know it we've created an expectation that we're always going to do it. To break a pattern of behaviour, you have to do something you wouldn't normally do. A delegated task is a great vehicle for changing the way you relate to a team member because it's easier to establish new ways of working together on a task that has no history for your team member. And, once you've done it on one task, it's a lot easier to change the way you relate to each other the rest of the time.

All adults are managers – we're just not all people managers

Everyone manages something at work . . . even if it's just themselves and the effect they have on other people. People use resources, information or equipment to do their jobs and manage their use. I mean, you can't even keep your papers sorted unless you manage your filing system. At work, there's always more to getting the task done than the bits the person does for themselves. There are contributions from other people to manage, people to be kept informed of progress, relationships with colleagues, customers and suppliers to be managed – and that's just for starters.

It's all about learning to let go

Shifting to adult/adult relationships isn't a skill shift because people are already doing it outside work and some of the time at work. It's an attitude shift. It's about managers letting go of the apron strings. Okay, it's hard at first (especially for us control freaks) but some ways of letting go are more comfortable than others and that's where agreeing a task management process comes in. I meant to ask you – how do the numbers stack up in your team between the people you leave alone to get on with things and the people you check up on?

Doing the task is the easy bit

We all have our favourite methods. I call mine the RAP method because when I say it out loud I think I sound like Will Smith of *Men in Black* fame (oh dear – delusional again). It goes like this – Explore, Focus, Plan, Do, Implement, Evaluate, Sustain and it's based on a series of questions that kick-start my brain into manual mode at each stage.

It's not the task, it's the task management that matters

When I delegate a task I want the team member who is doing it to:

- Have a clear understanding of what should be happening at all points in the process.
- Be on top of what is actually happening, even the bits they're getting other people to do.
- Be alert to anything that doesn't seem as it should, and to be prepared to investigate and take action to sort it out.
- Keep me fully informed of any developments, especially anything unusual or unpredicted but without making me feel like they're delegating upwards.

Too much to ask? I don't think so. When I share control (I never give it up, I can't stand the sleepless nights) I like to know exactly how the other person is going to do it and I want them to be absolutely clear where my responsibility ends and theirs begins. I'm not asking anything of them that I don't ask of myself. I expect to know what's going on with my tasks at any point in time – if only to keep the boss off my back. I bet the same applies to you.

What you focus on expands – so focus on task management

If, whenever you delegate a task, you make a point of asking a simple question (how are you going to ensure that what is supposed to happen actually does happen?) you'll soon get them into the habit of thinking 'task management'. If trust is believing in the absence of proof, a task management system is more like 'doveryay, no proveryay' (trust but verify) because at any time you can call for an update and test their task management system. And if it includes details of who needs to be consulted, informed, involved, etc., it means you won't be left dealing with the interpersonal sensitivities that can arise when someone gets left out of the loop!

Look after the inputs and the outputs will look after themselves

While they are thinking about the task and how to manage it (in other words being output, outcome and process driven) you can be thinking about them as employees and what they bring to the task (characteristics and other inputs) and how they can best use these to achieve the results.

Managing the person, not the task

Our biggest responsibility is to keep our staff in adult mode in their relationships with us and others. The single most important thing we can do to make that happen is to hold them responsible for the consequences of their actions and inactions. I'll explain this in more depth in Chapter 21 but, for now, let me assure you that I'm not talking about blame cultures. And I'm not saying that holding them responsible lets you off the hook completely. You are responsible for:

Our biggest responsibility is to keep our staff in adult mode in their relationships with us and others.

- Ensuring they have clarity about what they are doing – and I mean their own clarity, not just a half-baked version of yours. The acid test of clarity is when they can explain it to someone else.

- Managing the factors affecting their performance – which involves ensuring their way forward is clear of any obstacles that they can't manage for themselves.

- Encouraging, motivating and appreciating them – so they know they matter.

Helping them improve performance and make the most of their talents

The crucial thing with this responsibility is to understand how they use their characteristics to achieve their performance, seeing them in the round and helping them increase the ways in which they help and reduce the ways in which they hinder. You do this by:

- Ensuring they review their experience regularly – helping them learn how to observe themselves neutrally so they can see clearly the cause and effect relationships between their behaviour and their results.

- Helping them become ever more self-aware – because the more they know who they are, the more they can work with who they are, instead of wasting energy trying to be something they're not.

- Guiding them in developing their characteristics – with an emphasis on building from strength rather than eradicating weakness, by finding ways to exploit their helpful characteristics in new ways that compensate for gaps in their performance.

Empowering people to believe they can do more than they think they can

The best thing you can do to empower your staff is to help build their self-esteem. Treating them like adults is an excellent start. And it's about getting to know what's in their heads and helping them disentangle the helpful beliefs from the hindering beliefs. Most of all, it's about believing in their potential, even when they don't believe it themselves. You do this by:

It's about believing in their potential, even when they don't believe it themselves.

- Finding out what matters most to them – helping them identify what they feel passionately about at work and, because in the end we all want to matter, encouraging them to focus on ways they can make a difference.

- Expanding their reach – encouraging them to see that they are capable of more so they want to raise the bar to achieve more stretching goals.

- Encouraging them to be a positive influence on others – finding ways for them to have a wider and deeper influence on the people they interact with.

Delegation is a brilliant opportunity to manage, improve and empower

Like most overworked managers, I manage by exception, by which I mean I tend to get involved more when things go wrong than when they go right. The exception to this is when I delegate. Because someone is doing a task that's above their normal level of work, I take a lot more care to stay connected to them while they're doing it. And I milk it for all it's worth as a vehicle for managing, improving and empowering their performance. I find that team members enjoy taking on dele-gated tasks when they know they're going to get positive, one-to-one attention from the boss and the chance to shine.

IN SHORT

- **Treat people like adults and they'll start acting like adults.** Most people already treat some of their team like adults and some like children. What's the difference in the way they respond to you?

- **Get your team member to do the task *and* manage it.** What difference would it make to your team's performance if you could trust every team member to manage their own tasks without constant chasing?

- **Holding our team responsible for the things they do is the single biggest improvement we can make in the way we manage.** How might things be different in your team if you held everyone responsible, and not just the people you trust?

- **Focus on the person and get them to focus on the task.** If you started to tackle performance issues at source (by working on your team members' inputs) instead of at symptom level (the task itself), how might the way you manage change?

13

How do you analyze the dynamics for a particular task and team member?

Accessing all your knowledge and making the most of your team member

Kick-start your subconscious with a brain dump

The first problem we face when delegating is that, when we tell the team member what we think they need to know to do the task, we can only tell them what's in our conscious minds at the time. And that's likely to be task-specific knowledge because that's what we're focusing on. But we use a lot more than that when we do the task ourselves. We use all our experience – those pearls of wisdom and neat little insights into the way things work around here that are buried in our subconscious.

I've already said that accessing our subconscious isn't easy so I keep a checklist of questions that I've built up over the years to act as triggers for my subconscious. It's a pretty generic checklist so, if it works for you, you're welcome to use it – it's in Appendix 2 – and I use it as the basis for dumping stuff out of my head on to paper. Why not use it as a starter for ten and develop a checklist that suits you?

Get it out in raw data form not as briefing information

As with any brainstorm type activity, it's important not to judge or edit what's coming out (that comes later) but just get your thoughts down on paper. The beauty of an unstructured brain dump is that it uses your right brain, which more easily taps you into your subconscious. If you do something structured, you use your left brain which tends to keep you working with what's in your conscious mind.

Checklist questions will only take you so far

The checklist questions will take you over the surface of all the related issues but they won't necessarily get you into the depth of what you know. You do that by reading your notes and letting them act as a trigger in their own right. It helps to leave a few hours between the two rounds of brain dumping if you can.

It's just as important to know what you don't know as what you do

One of the beliefs that's served me well is that success depends more on knowing what you don't know than on what you do know. Most of my jobs have been change management focused so, I've tended to work in the gaps of my knowledge rather than in my comfort zone. I use the Kipling rhyme 'I keep six honest serving men, they taught me all I knew, their names are What and Where and When and How and Why and

Who?' as prompts to brainstorm all the questions a bright, inquisitive child might ask about the task. This gives me the naïve but cutting and oddly perceptive questions and keeps me from getting stale. I use the answers to add to my brain dump.

Separate the facts from the assumptions

Don't assume that everything you've brain dumped is fact. It may be assumption or a belief based on a misinterpreted experience. So, go through all the notes you've made and ask yourself the question 'how do I know that' to surface anything that might be an assumption based on experience rather than a fact. It's not a problem to work on assumptions (we all do it all the time) but it's always better to do it on manual (so your RAS is alert to counter-evidence) than on autopilot.

Surface your subconscious expectations

You'll have surfaced a lot of these in the last step (subconscious expectations are a kind of assumption) but also ask yourself 'how would I know my team member had done a good job?' And think back to some of the times you've been disappointed with what people have done for you and ask 'what disappointed me?' Add your notes to your brain dump.

Make the connections

Okay, time to sort, sift and get a sense of the dynamic. First, go through your notes and identify any trends, themes or connected bits of information and use them as headings to cluster the data together. (I do the brain dump straight on to the computer which makes this a 'cut-and-paste' task and I know some people who write their brain dump thoughts on post-its, then use a whiteboard to cluster them.) Don't use a standard list of headings (like task, people, organization) as it's too left-brain. Look at what your notes are telling you. For example, if you've made a lot of notes about the agendas of stakeholders and problems with red tape, 'sensitivities' might be a force affecting the dynamic. After you've understood the dynamic, sift out anything that no longer feels relevant. And that's it – you're done with the task!

Define competent performance of the task

If you know the person you need, you can make the most of the person you've got. In recruitment, we use a person specification to describe the person we need to the job and we get that from the job description – so start by thinking about what's involved in doing the task in this operating context. You might find it helpful to work from the notes you made when you analyzed the task. Then think about what characteristics (knowledge, attitudes, behaviours, skills including thinking skills) someone would need to do the task well. To help you get used to working with characteristics, Appendix 3 has some examples. Your list of required characteristics is your person specification for that task.

Assess your team member

Now, consider each characteristic in turn and identify where you think your performer lies on a continuum:

Needs a lot .... Uses this
of development well already

Somewhere just short of 'uses this well already' will be 'performance just needs fine-tuning'. If you know your team member well, you should be able to do this easily, but if in doubt, try identifying their most recent best and worst performance and thinking about what they did well and less well.

Get to the heart of the employee dynamic

Having the characteristics needed to perform well in a task and actually performing well are two different things, so this is the point at which you need to blend your knowledge of the task and your knowledge of your team member. It's part 'walkthrough' and part risk assessment and you do it by imagining your team member doing the task. Where are they most likely to struggle and where will they just sail through? And does that tie in with your assessment of their characteristics?

Think about compensatory characteristics

By now, you should be clear where the potential performance gaps are, but don't start identifying development action yet. Instead, think about how you can make the most of the characteristics your team member already uses well. For example, a team member of mine was pretty low on empathy, an important characteristic in a task I wanted to delegate to her. Her best characteristics were her logical and analytical skills and I thought she'd be fine if she used those skills to find the logic in their position and behaviour and to analyze the needs driving their behaviour.

Exploiting existing well-developed characteristics, by identifying new uses for them which compensate for less well-developed ones, is not only a good way of reducing risks, it's also a good way of building people up for the task ahead.

Design a radar system to manage the risks

You can't allow the task outputs and outcomes to suffer at the hands of a team member who needs development. From the development needs and risks you identified, think about what early warning signs you need to be on the look out for. Also, this is a good time to listen to your specific fears about delegating this task in case they generate anything for the radar system. In the example I'm using, lack of empathy risks interpersonal sensitivities and complaints. The early warning signals for this would be negative feedback from the people she was dealing with. Once you know what you're looking for, you need to work out how best to detect them. The question to ask is 'what information do I need (in what form, at which points, after what triggers) to know I need to intervene?' In my example, I needed to set up regular communication with stakeholders so I didn't have to rely on people seeking me out to tell me (you know yourself how easy it is to be the last person to know when a team member is generating negative feedback). Your radar system is complete when you've done this for all the risks and development needs.

The question to ask is 'what information do I need (in what form, at which points, after what triggers) to know I need to intervene?'.

If, when you're designing your radar system, you try to keep it neutral (in my example this means asking 'how are things going with my team member on that task?' rather than 'any problems?') you'll get the good stuff coming up on your radar as well as the early warning signs. And the good stuff is great to use in motivating, encouraging and appreciating.

IN SHORT

▶ **Get your subconscious knowledge and expectations out on the table too.** What could you do to trigger all the wisdom you have in your subconscious?

▶ **Make sure you know what's fact and what's an assumption.** What have you taken as fact in the past, only to discover, at an awkward moment that it was only an assumption?

▶ **Find the common themes and issues so you know what matters most.** What kinds of connections do you see that you know your team member wouldn't?

▶ **Work out the gaps between your team member and the ideal performer of the task.** In an ideal world, what kind of person would you delegate to and where does your team member not measure up?

▶ **Get the best out of whatever your team member has going for them.** What do they bring to their work that adds special value and how can you exploit that in the way they do the delegated task?

▶ **Your people management will only be as good as your radar system.** How do you ensure you're tipped off before your team member gets into irretrievable trouble?

14

How do you come to a shared understanding of the task?

The briefing discussion – dealing with the issue of perspective

Getting them to ask and answer the two meta-questions

In an adult/adult relationship, your team member is responsible for getting their own clarity about the task, so it's better if you don't make all the running in the briefing session. I get them to prepare by answering what I call the two meta-questions:

- What questions do I need to ask to get clarity about this task?

- Where, or from whom, can I get answers to those questions?

The first meta-question isn't the same as asking 'what do I need to know to get clarity on this task?' because that question takes them into a different kind of thinking – it's like starting with the answers and working back to the question –

and you need your team member to be in analytical not judging mode. The second meta-question is about ensuring your team member realizes that no one person is the fount of all wisdom on a particular subject or task (which takes the heat off you).

Then meet and explore the task and its operating context

I like to use this discussion to work through my team member's questions and I use my brain dump notes to help me answer rather than as a structure for the meeting. I mark each piece of information as I give it so that, if their questions have missed anything, I can add it at the end. I also use my headings to explain the main forces in the dynamic. A discussion like this will take more time than a 'tell and sell' briefing but it'll pay great dividends later on.

Surfacing assumptions and subconscious expectations

We've already discussed analyzing behaviour and the same approach will serve you well in this discussion. If you listen for what your team member is implying by what they're saying (as well as to what they're actually saying), you'll pick up clues about their beliefs, assumptions and subconscious expectations. And if you take a 'wondering' approach (for example, 'when you said that, it sounded like you believe this – is that right?') you can test understanding and get things to the surface that might otherwise affect results.

Get them to write up the notes of the discussion

This doesn't just save you a task, it's a great way of testing understanding. Before I started doing this, I had many a discussion where I thought that we had a shared understanding only to find we were using two different languages (it reminded me of being in Australia). Check your team member is writing up the notes in their own words, and look out for repetition of your words or any other indicators that they don't have their own insight.

Once they're clear on the task, move on to their performance

It'll be easier for your team member if they've got a good grasp of the outcome, output and process parts of the task before they have to think of the inputs so I like to have the task and the person discussions separately, although at a pinch you can do them together. You can ask them to prepare by analyzing the task themselves the way you did in the last step in the process or, if you think they aren't yet self-aware enough to do that, you can use your preparation as a structure for the discussion. It works well either way as long as you remember to:

- Keep everything neutral and non-judgemental – talk about the needs of the task and if you are talking about a characteristic that might hinder performance, remember to balance that by giving an example of where it works well so that your team member feels analyzed not criticized.

- Put forward your thoughts on compensatory characteristics, development gaps, risks and so on as thoughts not tablets of stone – and ask for your team member's thoughts and listen to the answers.

■ Make sure you discuss the standards of performance you expect – not just in terms of practicalities and characteristics but how you'd like them to behave.

Don't forget to agree the ground rules – they affect the planning process

Apart from a shared understanding of the task, this is the time when you need to establish the ground rules for things like:

■ How often, and in what form, you want to be kept informed.

■ What decisions you want to reserve to yourself, or have taken in discussion with you, rather than have taken by your team member alone.

■ What authority and limits your team member will have.

■ Under what kind of circumstances you will intervene.

IN SHORT

▶ **They need their own clarity so get them to do the work.** In your experience, what's different about people who really know what they're doing compared to people who don't?

▶ **Remember to discuss both the task and their performance of it.** What matters most to you about the way your team member does the task?

▶ **Get your ground rules in place early.** What kinds of things do you need to put in place to help you feel secure about delegating?

15

How do you help your team member get the task and task management processes right?

The planning discussion and the use of report backs and checkpoint discussions

Start with a 'walkthrough' to be clear about what should happen at each stage

I described a 'walkthrough' in Chapter 6 so I won't repeat it here. Use it to get them thinking in more detail than was possible in your previous discussions about what should be happening at each point in the process.

Pretend to be the other people involved to get a fuller picture

During the 'walkthrough' it's important to remember that different stakeholders will have different perspectives. Including them in the walkthrough is a great opportunity to try to see the task from their perspective. If your team member describes, for example, the distribution of a customer survey, the 'walkthrough' should describe that from the recipient's perspective too.

Taping the 'walkthrough' gives a great resource for detailed planning

Because you get the detail as well as the big picture from doing a 'walkthrough', I like to tape the discussion (it's the only use I make of my Dictaphone) so my team member can use it to fill out the detail in his task plan. I have a task diary (an A4 size day per page type) where I keep my 'should be happening' notes for all my hands-on tasks (those for which I'm responsible for the task management process) written against the day they are due to be done. I use the weekend pages for tasks that don't need to be done on a specific day but do need to be completed that week.

Now for task management – radar first

The two questions to ask that will help you design the early warning radar system are:

- What do you have to put in place so that you know if what is supposed to be happening is actually happening?
- How will you know that what is being produced is of the right quality?

The radar system doesn't have to be particularly sophisticated, although it does have to include everything you picked up in the risks discussion. When we implemented the appraisal system we asked for plans with names and dates for training and appraisal; our task management process consisted of getting statistics on people trained and appraised so we could compare it to plan (at least, it did eventually!). To ensure quality, we issued feedback surveys and followed up on any negative feedback in discussion with the trainers and senior managers.

You need the right radar system to get the right feedback to adjust

I had a colleague who used to manage a repeating process that took place over several months and involved major inputs from several people. A single activity in the process could have a deadline of six weeks. Before we reviewed it, her task management system involved sending a reminder to the person who was doing the task, a few days before the deadline was up. Because the people she was getting the input from were overworked managers, her reminder usually served to kickstart the exercise from scratch with poor-quality results. When we reviewed her task management process, I asked her to break down the overall task into smaller tasks and identify what needed to be done on a week-by-week basis. She gave this breakdown to the people doing the task and asked them for a short email progress report at the end of each week. If the progress report didn't arrive or if, on reading it, she picked up variations between what was supposed to have been done that week and what had been done, she was able to get on to it straight away. That's what a good radar system gives you.

Task management also includes stakeholder management

In addition to the radar system, task management needs to include activities related to managing stakeholder relationships. Who needs to be involved and kept informed and at what stages? It's important to include this because communication and involvement will generate activities (meetings, progress reports) that are not directly required for the production of the outputs (and so may not have made it on to the task plan) but which are crucial for the achievement of outcomes like customer satisfaction.

Tasks, like justice must be done *and* seen to be done

You may not be doing the task now that you've delegated it, but it can't just disappear into a black hole. You need to know it's all going well (as opposed to hoping no news is good news) which is where regular report-backs come in. Report-backs need only be 5 minute face-to-face updates or short emails but they're a vital part of your people management early warning radar system so they need to happen.

Finding the checkpoints – the critical moments of choice on which success turns

Tasks, once started, tend to generate their own momentum as do the people doing them. Beyond the quick report-backs, you need to set up checkpoints at those critical moments in the process when decisions are needed. Checkpoints are different from interim deadlines which come too late for intervention or rather for the kind that doesn't involve major rework. An interim deadline is likely to be the point at which a report is written or a meeting takes place, so checkpoints need to be when the decisions are taken on what to put into the report or on the agenda. It's not just ease of intervention that makes it sensible to have discussion at these times, it's ease of influencing your team member during their decision-making process – which is better than overruling them or picking up the pieces afterwards.

Building in enough time for the right kind of checkpoint discussion

Checkpoint discussions help you pick up potential input issues, alert you to the need to intervene, and give you a chance to check whether the clarity you and your team member had at the beginning is still valid or whether it needs adjusting on the basis of your team member's experience of doing the task.

To achieve these aims, you need to listen for anything that generates your 'off' feeling. I use checkpoint discussions to encourage people to trust their own intuition by asking them to tell me about anything that's happened since our last checkpoint discussion that has made them feel 'off' – or, if they're not that self-aware, I get the same results by asking them what's been irritating them lately. I know that it takes longer, but if you get them to tell you the story in 'narrative-rich' form, you can get a sense of how they felt and it's easier for your internal radar system to work.

You need to listen for anything that generates your 'off' feeling.

Narrative-rich discussions are where you basically get them to tell you the whole story of the event. If you get them to give you the little details, the nuances, their feelings, you can pick up so much more about what's happening than you can with a bullet point summary or a 'just give me the hard facts' approach.

If they tend to stick to the facts, just ask questions to open them up a bit. In a fast-paced world, people are conditioned against 'rambling' in meetings with their boss but 'narrative-rich' discussions leave you with as much insight as if you'd done the task yourself. This is a great help when it comes to giving your own input and testing the soundness of their judgement (not to mention making your team member feel really good about getting all that attention). So, ensure your team member builds enough time into their plan.

Putting it all into one big plan

Add any activities related to implementing the radar system, stakeholder management, report-backs and checkpoint discussions into the task plan so that your team member has all their tasks on one plan. This means they can settle into a task-focused comfort zone knowing they're still covering all the bases.

IN SHORT

▶ **Use 'walkthroughs' to be clear about what should be happening.** What do you do to ensure your team member is clear about every stage of the task process?

▶ **Help them get the best radar system they can.** What added value can you bring to the development of their radar system?

▶ **Manage at the critical moments of choice.** Can you look at any task and know when the key decision points will be?

▶ **Make time to listen to their experience of doing the task.** When was the last time you made time to sit down with someone and asked them to tell you all about it?

16

How do you help them learn from their experience?

The review for learning discussion – gaining valuable insight from the experience

Distance lends perspective

If you dealt with issues as they arose during the task and if you got through the sometimes heated ramifications of holding your team member responsible for their actions, then by the time you get to the review for learning there won't be any emotion and defensiveness left. On the contrary, there'll be that lovely sense of perspective that you get once there's been some water under the bridge – and, of course, a lot of cool thinking and neutral analysis. The insight you both get from the review can be on a number of levels – knowledge, skills, experience, expertise, attitudes, beliefs, etc. – but all of them bring a heightened sense of self-awareness that will help your team member perform better in the future.

Getting out of manager mode into neutral observer mode

The best way to help your team member learn from their experience is to take an 'equal learning partners' approach.

Listen carefully for beliefs that hinder performance.

This involves being a neutral observer when they're giving you their analysis and insight and listening carefully for beliefs that hinder performance and anything that needs reframing.

The review for learning approach

Before the review for learning takes place, your team member should use the questions in Chapter 7 as a framework for thinking about their performance, making notes of any points they wish to raise in discussion. At this stage, their notes are intended for personal use in the discussion, as experience shows that sharing the notes in advance encourages defensiveness which inhibits the quality of discussion. The aim of the meeting is to come to a shared understanding about your team member's performance of the task. Following the meeting, the team member should write up a note of the discussion, using the questions as headings and give the manager a copy.

Helping them stop judging and start analyzing

When I do review for learning meetings with members of my team, I find they're pretty hard on themselves. It always seems easier for them to find their failings than their talents. In some ways, it makes my job easy because all I have to do is find the bits they're not seeing. The chances are that your team member's answers to these questions will be of the black and white variety. Try to keep the analysis around inputs rather than outcomes or outputs, as the latter can be ascribed to factors beyond the team member's control and you could just end up debating the results, which defeats the object.

Giving them another perspective to consider

I remember a review with a team member who said he struggled with keeping twenty-seven plates in the air at once and that he really wished he could focus on one task at a time and get a good run at it. He believed he had no other option but to adapt to his job. Now, the plus side of being a control freak is that you don't think there's anything you can't control, so I suggested he tried getting the job to adapt to his needs instead. It had never occurred to him but we talked through a few ideas he could try, including blocking out a half day each week with no interruptions so he could focus on one task. Sounds obvious when I tell the story, I know, but that's the point of telling the story. Reframing isn't rocket science, it's just about looking at something from a different angle and, as you're not your team member, you're just doing what comes naturally.

Reframing isn't rocket science, it's just about looking at something from a different angle.

Encourage them to want to raise the bar

If you handle things properly, they'll come out like a high jumper who wants to raise the bar next time around.

IN SHORT

- **Before you move on, take stock to get at all the experiential learning.** How often do you sit down with your team member and review their experience with them to extract the lessons?

- **Help them get a balanced view of their experience.** Do you find yourself tempering their judgements of their performance with the wisdom of your broader perspective?

- **Leave them wanting to do even better next time.** How do you think they feel after they've completed a delegated task for you?

Knowing when to step in and when to stand back

▶ Every potential intervention is a moment of choice

Every time you have to decide whether or not to intervene, you are making a choice that will either empower or limit your team member. It's in these moments of choice that you will create an adult/adult or parent/child relationship.

▶ Being alert to the triggers

If you've followed the process in Part 2, you'll already have checkpoint discussions in place ahead of the key decision points. This then takes care of one of the triggers . . . at least for the foreseen decisions. You are reliant on your radar system to give you early warning of the unforeseen decisions as well as of the times when you need to take development action, manage factors affecting performance, deal with variations, hold your team member responsible for correcting a mistake, or give them encouragement, motivation or appreciation.

▶ Don't just take my word for it – check it against your own experience

As you read this part think back to your last experience of delegation and your experience of intervening and review it against what you're reading.

17

When do they need development?

The need to help them when they're being stretched

You've already anticipated some development needs

Before you can think about how to improve performance, you need to be sure you're targeting the right area (who has time for misdirected effort these days?). The trainers on my team have told me countless horror stories about people attending the wrong courses (and, no, I don't mean they turned up at the wrong event!). Going on a meetings skills course when they needed assertiveness is a waste of everyone's time.

Generic training courses can't focus like coaching can

Most skills are a combination of a number of characteristics and poor performance is rarely the result of problems with all the component characteristics.

You're **skilled** when you can consistently produce your desired effect. Some people would argue that if you make someone feel snubbed, for example, you do not have good interpersonal skills. I say that if that's what you intended, then you're skilled and if it's not what you intended, you're not.

With my background in individual and organizational development, I feel bad about saying it, but I really don't think training courses are the answer to developing people. For one thing, they tend to be generic in nature – e.g. communication skills, meetings skills – so, they don't have time to cover all the component characteristics. For another, the participants have to sit through a lot of stuff they're already good at to get to the bit they need – assuming, of course, that it gets covered.

But the biggest problem with training courses is they create dangerous expectations. I've seen too many managers send team members on courses and (a) expect them to come back 'cured' and (b) think it's the trainer's responsibility to develop their team, not theirs. Single characteristic training (e.g. questioning, listening) can help but, given that learning comes from experience, it's never going to replace a manager's role in developing the team.

As with managing, the key to developing people is understanding performance

To understand exactly where you need to focus your development attention, you need to repeat the analysis of characteristics you did for the person specification but dig a bit deeper. Let's say your initial analysis concluded that their meeting skills needed development. Start by identifying someone you know who has excellent meetings skills and ask 'What do they bring to their performance?' Don't be surprised if you end up with a long list (I've done this exercise with lots of people and once they get into it, they really motor) including questioning, listening, influencing, summarizing, empathizing, dealing with difficult people, confidence, assertiveness, spoken communication, clarifying, testing understanding, building support and facilitating.

No one needs development in a whole skill area

No one who has problems in meetings will have problems with all the component characteristics. So, when you assess your team member against each of the characteristics involved in the skill (which is the next step), you'll find the ones where they do need development. Use the continuum idea we discussed earlier to assess your team member against each characteristic in your definition of competent performance.

I've laboured the wasted time in getting development wrong, but there's another reason for getting the analysis right . . . the self-esteem of your team member. Compare how you'd feel if your boss told you that your meetings skills need development with the way you would feel if they said they'd analyzed your performance in meetings and felt it wasn't doing justice to your ability and that it was only your questioning skills that were hindering you and that everything else was excellent. They'd be telling you, you're already 90 per cent there. No matter what their logic tells them, most people subconsciously associate development with an admission of weakness, so the

There's another reason for getting the analysis right . . . the self-esteem of your team member.

smaller the 'admission' they have to make, the better they feel.

Create a homoeopathic development opportunity

Once you know what you're developing, you need to create a good development opportunity. I use what I call the homoeo-pathic development method (a little of what kills you cures you, but make sure it's well diluted and carefully managed). This is a far cry from 'getting back on the horse that threw you', which can be psychologically damaging. However, the homoeopathic method does require facing up to the issue, because avoidance makes the problem seem bigger to the sub-conscious than it is. It means finding a safe way to allow your team member the opportunity to develop their characteristic. Team meetings can be the most comfortable environment to practise in, so try to exploit their development potential with regular presentations, giving other people the chair for items, etc.

Do enough reviews for learning

We've already talked about these so I won't repeat myself here. What I will say is this. A famous American sports coach said that the game isn't over until you've learned everything it has to teach you. That's fine when there's a gap between 'games' but when does that happen at work? People can't learn from an experience they haven't reviewed, so be respon-sible for making sure they can find the time.

IN SHORT

- **No one is hopeless at a whole skill area**. Do you look at whole skill areas when you're developing your people or do you see the nuances of performance?

- **Time spent targeting the right development need now pays real dividends later**. Have you ever sent someone on the wrong course?

- **Managed properly, a little of what kills them will cure them**. Do you let people avoid the situations where they perform poorly? Do you push them too hard to get back on the horse?

18

When are there things that only you can do?

The need to manage factors affecting their performance

We think nothing of being a step in a colleague's process

I'm guessing you don't have a problem providing an input to the task of, say, a colleague in another department. I'm also guessing that when called upon to provide your input, you do it without thinking about managing their task for them. After all, that's their job; you're just one of the people they coordinate. So why should it be different when the person doing the task management and coordinating your input is your team member? There are two ways you can be a step in a team member's process:

- You can be one of the people with an input to make to a task they are managing.

- You can have responsibility for managing a factor affecting their performance.

Some things will always be your job

Many managers tell me they can't delegate tasks because one of the things it involves is, for example, authorizing expenditure, which has to be done at their level. Rubbish, there's nothing to stop a manager in that position delegating the task and becoming a step in their team member's task process (the authorizing expenditure step). Of course, I accept that there are some tasks that a manager should never delegate – in fact I'd insist managers keep all people management tasks to themselves – but this isn't one of them.

Retaining one element of a delegated task is fine as long as you don't retain the task management responsibility. Just as it would be with any other colleague, it's got to be down to your team member to make sure you do what you are supposed to do when you are supposed to do it. There's an extra development benefit in delegating this kind of task. Your team member gets to practise upward management, which will help them develop skills in dealing with managers who are more senior to them, and you get to observe first-hand how they handle it, which adds a unique dimension to your knowledge of your team member.

> **Retaining one element of a delegated task is fine as long as you don't retain the task management responsibility.**

Managing factors affecting performance

There will be times when your team member hits a problem in doing the task that they genuinely can't resolve. For example, if a project is overrunning and something else has to give way, your team member won't have the authority to make that decision no matter what autonomy you've given them about the task. A word of caution before you leap in to help; make sure the factor is genuinely beyond their control and there are good reasons why your intervention is needed. If you're anything like me, any excuse to take over can look like a good enough reason.

The conflict between developing people and delivering the task

Of course, it's not always a black and white decision. Sometimes, you know perfectly well that they could do it themselves, given time. However, time isn't something either of you have, and it would be far quicker if you just got it sorted so your team member could move forward. The bottom line is we're all employed to deliver results and whilst the advice in this book is all about improving our capacity to do exactly that, obviously there will be times when the short-term need has to take precedence over the longer-term need. As it happens, the more we invest in improving capacity in the longer term, the fewer problems we have to worry about on a day-to-day basis, but that's no comfort now, when you're up against it. If in doubt, do what is best for the task and promise yourself you'll find your team member another way to learn what they've missed this time.

Don't rush the 'I'll deal with it' decision

Remember though, that I said 'if in doubt'. Given the price you're paying in terms of a lost opportunity for developing performance, you owe it to your team member to ensure your decision is a considered one, not a knee-jerk reaction. Make sure the strength of learning opportunity (will they learn something really useful if they try to do it themselves?) really doesn't outweigh the time commitment (will they have to spend a lot of time to achieve something that will take you only minutes?). And don't give up before you've tried brainstorming ways of getting the best of both worlds.

People judge you on your responses to your day-to-day moments of choice

I've yet to come across a decision that, in the final analysis, wasn't an on-balance decision. We make our choices and take the downside with the upside. Bear in mind though, the consequences aren't just the ones to do with the issue of substance, they're also the ones to do with the impression you make on people as a manager.

IN SHORT

- **You can be a step in their process**. Can your ego cope with them managing you for a change?

- **Manage the factors affecting their performance but not their task**. Are you doing everything you can to remove obstacles that are beyond their control?

- **Don't step in without thinking through all the consequences**. Do you intervene to help or do you just take over when things are going off course?

19

When are the key decision-making points?

The need to challenge thinking and keep them focused on outcomes

Getting attached to the task

The characteristics you admire about your team member – their motivation, complete ownership of the task and commitment to achieving the outputs – are often the very ones that hinder their judgement process. How? By making them feel attached to the task when good judgement requires them to be detached. It's a tough decision for anyone who's invested heavily in something, to accept that the best way forward is to abandon what they've done and start again. It's even tougher if they're emotionally attached. Remember, you both agreed the outputs and process needed to produce the outcomes *before* the task got started, so you need to stay open so you can use insight from your experience to adjust course and/or destination.

Using checkpoints to keep on track or change the track

You scheduled your checkpoint discussions at the planning stage and we've talked about listening for things that give you an 'off' feeling. But what do you do when you've heard something? Two things:

- Challenge their thinking – help them think their way from symptom to root cause and from options to consequences.

- Refocus them – when they're focusing on outputs, remind them of outcomes and when they are locked into their own narrow perspective, remind them of stakeholder perspectives.

It's all a matter of asking the right questions

You do both of these by asking questions, but getting the right question to unlock someone's thinking is a skill in its own right. Imagine a team member comes to you seeking your agreement to their proposal. You want to be assured they've come up with the best way forward but you don't want to get bogged down in their task.

Getting the right question to unlock someone's thinking is a skill in its own right.

- If you simply ask *'Is that the best way forward?'* are they going to say no? Unlikely!

- Suppose you decide to probe a bit further by asking them *'Why is that the best way forward?'* Someone intelligent can make any solution look good and even convince you into believing they used the same intelligence to arrive at the solution in the first place!

■ If, however, you ask *'What other options did you consider and reject before deciding this was the best way forward?'* then they will have to talk you through their thinking process. You'll see not only whether they've been rigorous in their thinking but whether they have, indeed, chosen the best option.

Resist the temptation to answer your own questions

The key to effective intervention during these key decision points is to ask the questions then resist the temptation to answer them yourself in the form of advice. You can give input, of course, anything you know that will help them, but don't lead.

And to make their decisions for them

In all fairness, you can't hold someone responsible for the consequences of their decisions if they were just your decisions in disguise. If you're unhappy with the direction of their thinking, say something to change the input side of the decision-making equation – by working with them to reframe their analysis or by adding your own input, something you know but they don't.

And to save them from the consequences of their decisions

A 'walkthrough' is the best way I know of getting someone to see the consequences of their decision before they've caused any damage to the task. I use the questioning element of the 'walkthrough' as a way of getting them to see for themselves what I can see. Of course, you have the right to overrule their decision to protect the task; but see that for what it is – a failure.

My two favourite questions to unlock stuck thinking

When people can only see the constraints, I ask the big 'what if' questions. It's a way of tricking the mind but it works. I worked with a team who complained that central government set the agenda for their work and that this left them powerless to control their own destiny. I asked 'What if central government didn't exist?' They humoured me and came up with some excellent ideas. Then I asked, 'What if we could manage the constraint and do what you want to do?' The constraint is still there but now it isn't dominating their thinking and, because they are clear about what they want to achieve, they're more motivated to look for ways to manage around it. Try it and see.

When people can only see the constraints, I ask the big 'what if' questions.

IN SHORT

- **Challenge their thinking and keep them focused on outcomes.** What do you do to help people improve their decision making?

- **Ask questions to unblock their thinking but don't do their thinking for them.** Do you ask questions or just tell them what you think?

- **Don't make their decisions for them and don't save them from the consequences.** How do you react when you think your team member is making the wrong decisions?

20

When is what's actually happening not what should be happening?

The need to act when you pick up a variation or when they need your insight

Ignorance is never bliss

I was reading an article about great leaders in the Sunday paper a while back which made a telling point about the difference between leaders who succeeded and those who failed. Leaders who failed wouldn't allow anyone to give them bad news. It reminded me of a time when two junior staff didn't tell one of my managers about a problem because, and I quote, they 'didn't want to bother her as she was so busy'. Believe me, she wasn't half as busy as she became when she finally found out the full extent of the problem and had to do heaps of rework to get it back on track.

And neither is denial

Being an effective manager means dealing with things as they are, not as we'd like them to be. I have a friend with more potential than anyone I know but she doesn't trust her ability to cope with reality so she denies the existence of issues. In doing so, she creates experiences which reinforce her lack of self-belief. Reality can only be denied for so long – sooner or later, it has to be faced and the longer it's left, the tougher it gets. But it's not just about dealing with problems when they're smaller and more manageable (though that is an excellent philosophy). It's about what dealing with problems does for our self-confidence and self-belief. Mental muscles are just like any other muscle – the more we use them, the stronger they get. And the stronger they get, the fewer things faze us.

Being an effective manager means dealing with things as they are, not as we'd like them to be.

Variations are a chance to challenge your assumptions

Variations (something that isn't happening that should be; something that is happening that shouldn't be; or an unforeseen hazard on your radar screen) can be a real blessing in disguise. Variations don't care how busy we are. They make us stop and think anyway and that's something we tend not to do enough of in the normal course of daily events. And in that 'stopping and thinking time', if we suspend our natural irritation at being knocked off track and really listen to what the variation is telling us, it can make all the difference to the success of the task.

So why make it hard for people to give you bad news?

Looked at from this perspective, there's no such thing as bad news – just an opportunity to surface assumptions and make adjustments if they're needed. Try to get a reputation with staff that they can tell you anything without you losing it. Flying on manual (using variations as a chance to rethink and be sure you're on the right course) instead of autopilot gives you a chance to add your unique value to the team's work. Besides, dealing with variations is easy:

1. Establish the root cause of the variation.
2. Challenge existing expectations of what should be happening to see if they need to change (new destination).
3. Identify options for action either to get back on track or to change the expectations of what should be happening.
4. Decide which is best and implement.
5. Go back to watching the radar screen.

In the appraisal example I've been talking about throughout the book, with some departments we took action to close the gap between actual and plan and with others we amended the original plans because they'd been overambitious. These actions took the pressure off the managers who were implementing appraisal and made the implementation smoother. Yet we'd never have reviewed those plans if we hadn't picked up the variation.

You can't solve problems at the same level of thinking that created them

The way we label a problem often inadvertently restricts us in our search for a solution. One of my earliest management jobs was helping a manager who had a problem with his organizational structure. I read the file to get the background and I learned that there had been seven structure reviews in the last ten years, none of which had improved the working of the team. They weren't bad structures, so I decided to focus not on structure but on performance. To cut a long story short, they were trying to fix a people management problem with a structural solution for which no structural solution was possible.

IN SHORT

- **Get a reputation for not killing the messenger.** How do you react when people bring you bad news?

- **Be positive about the value of variations.** Do you get irritated when something doesn't go according to plan or do you see it as an opportunity?

- **Get to a new level of thinking to solve problems.** Do you challenge all your assumptions about a problem before you set out to solve it?

21

When are they not taking responsibility?

The need to hold them responsible for putting things right when they go wrong

A healthy kind of discomfort

You get blamed but you take responsibility – one is externally imposed, the other internally generated. People who blame are avoiding taking their share of the responsibility by making someone else the bad guy. It's possible to create a culture that isn't a blame culture but which still expects people to put their mistakes right.

There's no avoiding the fact that a responsibility culture can be just as uncomfortable to work in as a blame culture – at the point at which the mistake is made. It's uncomfortable for whoever made the mistake, obviously, but also uncomfortable for the manager. But there the similarity ends. In a blame culture people just feel bad, whereas in a responsibility culture they feel bad *and* get a chance to feel better by redeeming the situation. In a responsibility culture, the 'sanctioner' (the manager) is part of the sanction because they share responsibility for the mistake the team member makes. This last point is crucial to the success of a responsibility culture and to the use of sanctions because it's what gives the inherent fairness.

You need to take your share of the responsibility – no more and no less

If one of your team makes a mistake, then yes you are responsible because on one level that's the essence of your job – to be responsible for the performance of the people you manage. It's tough, but there's no getting away from it. The problem with the parent/child way of working is that the manager ends up taking all the responsibility. And where does that leave the team member who made the mistake? Letting the manager take the responsibility – that's where.

The problem with the parent/child way of working is that the manager ends up taking all the responsibility.

But what about some of those legendary delegators of your experience? Where do they stand on the responsibility issue? I knew a manager who delegated so much, she was able to spend large portions of her day reading – sometimes management magazines to be sure, but usually novels hidden inside the covers of a management magazine. Scratch the surface of a delegator like this and you'll find someone playing the child in the parent/child relationship. I bet too you won't have to look far to find the team member who's playing the parent and taking all the responsibility.

Creating a responsibility culture

When a mistake happens, the first thing to do is to ensure both you and the team member understand what's gone wrong and why. Understanding the cause and effect chain helps with generating solutions and gives insight for learning. Be factual and analytical not judgemental – blaming is counter-productive, generating defensiveness and loss of resilience, neither of which help your team's performance. And blaming people almost never makes people feel responsible but it can give them a way to avoid focusing on themselves, by being able to moan about having a bad boss instead.

We don't learn from mistakes that don't cost us anything

When our subconscious is filing our experience, it looks at the effect we've created to decide whether it belongs in the drawer marked 'pleasure' (let's see how many times we can do that again) or 'pain' (be afraid, be very afraid) and adjusts our future behaviour accordingly. In people with a normal survival instinct, avoiding pain is more important to our subconscious that getting pleasure, so anything that doesn't generate pain gets filed in the pleasure drawer.

I know it sounds horribly 'spare the rod' Victorian to say it, but the appropriate use of sanctions is critical to effective performance management. Sanctions must:

- Make it absolutely clear what was done wrong and why it was wrong.
- Be appropriate to the mistake.
- Be implemented on an adult/adult basis – i.e. shared.
- Give the chance for redemption by correcting the mistake, alleviating the consequences or learning a lesson for the future.

The best sanctions give people a chance to feel good again

They may hide it with bravado, but most people feel bad when they get it wrong, usually to the extent that they feel responsible – which depends on whether they operate mostly in parent mode (taking too much responsibility), child mode (taking too little) or adult mode (taking their share). We all want to feel good about ourselves – it's a basic psychological driver – and giving them the opportunity to put things right is crucial.

Discharge your share of responsibility by helping them find a solution

You can help your team member identify what outcomes they want (task back on course and amends made to those affected) and what ways *they* can bring those outcomes about. Whatever you do to help, don't add to their misery by taking the problem off them. It's the most psychologically emasculating thing you can do.

IN SHORT

- **Create a responsibility culture not a blame culture.** How do you think your team would describe the way you react when things go wrong?
- **Give them a chance to put things right.** Do you inadvertently reward people who make mistakes by taking the problem off them?
- **Help them find solutions that make them feel good.** Do you work with the person who has made the mistake to find ways they can make amends?

22

When do they need motivation, encouragement and appreciation?

The need to provide emotional support without becoming a crutch

If in doubt, ask – and remember to be in doubt more often

Encouragement, motivation and appreciation are intensely personal things so it's crazy to make assumptions. In all honesty, there's no substitute for direct learning about what works for your team member. Try asking them:

- What was your best ever experience of being encouraged (or motivated or appreciated, whichever one you're trying to find out about)?

- What was good about it? (Ask follow-up questions so they tell you in 'rich-narrative' form.)

- What was the most important thing, the one thing that really made the experience what it was?

And if you want to know what turns them off, ask about their worst experience too. Meanwhile, here are a few things that complement the basic psychology of human nature.

The best motivation is self-motivation

Trying to motivate someone who can't get themselves motivated is like giving someone aspirin for a headache caused by tense shoulders. They'll work in the short term but if the tense shoulders remain, you'll be stuck with supplying constant repeat prescriptions. Instead, try a more systemic approach – namely, generating self-motivation. Explore what matters most to them and help them find ways to make it more central to their work or to reframe their experience of work so they can see a clearer connection to what matters most.

Try a more systemic approach – namely, generating self-motivation.

Don't invalidate their feelings

Have you noticed the kind of things people say to encourage you when you're discouraged – things like 'you can do it' or 'it's not that bad'? And have you thought about what they're actually doing when they respond like this when you say 'I can't do it' or 'things couldn't get any worse'? They're saying 'you're wrong'. As if feeling discouraged isn't enough to cope with! People need to know they are understood and accepted, so pay attention to what they're saying so they feel heard.

I find the best way to move them forward is to suspend your judgement about whether they are right or wrong, exaggerating or distorting and start from where they are. Our beliefs create our experience so if they believe they've got a problem, then they've got a problem, so you might as well take it seriously. This doesn't mean you can't use some gentle humour if they're catastrophizing, as long as you do it in the course of helping them solve the problem. I know that what I'm about to say sounds horribly low EQ (emotional intelligence), but I've found that treating emotional issues like feelings of discouragement the same way as you'd treat a task-based problem really works.

I want to **distinguish emotions from feelings.** Emotions are mental states (coming from our thoughts) and feelings are physical sensations. Emotions can generate feelings as with anger and a tight feeling in the chest but they are separate. The same feeling can be associated with two emotions – for example, a churning stomach can be fear or excitement depending on our thoughts about the situation we're in.

So, help them establish the root cause and work to address it. You'll find that once they have a plan of attack, they'll feel in control again and that's half the battle with discouragement.

Believe in them even when they don't believe in themselves

When people are struggling, which often happens at some point during a delegated task, the first thing that suffers is their self-confidence and self-belief. Believing in someone doesn't mean you think they're perfect – it's not Pollyanna stuff. It comes from knowing who they are, what they're capable of doing and how they constrain themselves. Whatever you do, don't pretend you believe in them when you don't because their subconscious will pick up the incongruence in no time. Look for what you know to be fundamentally true about each team member (the thing that makes them worth knowing) and use that as the foundation of your belief in them. We all have an innate potential to grow beyond our constraints. Do what you can to help them do that.

Don't give praise, give feedback – to strengthen their internal validation system

Relying on feedback from others to know whether you've done something good or bad is a very risky business – reliance is a close friend of dependence. Besides, people praise and withhold praise for all sorts of reasons that tell you more about them than you. I use neutral feedback so team members can come to their own conclusions about their performance. A matter-of-fact approach – but one highly observant of the detail of their performance – tells them that you've really *seen* what they've done. This will not only please them but help them become more self-reliant and have more trust in their own judgement. And that'll help them deal with negative feedback too.

Reliance is a close friend of dependence.

IN SHORT

- **Don't do as you would be done by**. Does your approach to motivation, encouragement and appreciation reflect your own preferences?

- **Be a factual observer who records your team members' greatest moments**. Would your team members say that you really see their performance?

▶ **Believe in them even when they don't believe in themselves.** Can you find one thing in each of your team members that you can really believe in when the doubts are mounting?

■ *real* management for the way it is ■

Conclusion

▶ Leaving the hard sell until last

I think almost every book I've read on delegation starts by selling you the benefits, presumably to motivate you to try delegating. It seems more logical to me to assume that you're already motivated, otherwise you wouldn't have bought the book.

▶ Do you want the benefits enough to face up to the complexity?

Not sure? Then read on . . .

23

Why should you persevere with *real* delegating when it's so complex?

I can't answer that, I can only tell you why I persevere

Only you can know why you bought this book and what it would take to motivate you to try some of the ideas I'm putting forward. All I can do is tell you what motivates me to delegate and what I get out of it.

It enables you to shift your focus

The single best move any overworked manager can make is to shift focus from the tasks and outputs, to team members and inputs. Delegating enables you to do that. The less hands-on work you keep to yourself, the more time you have for managing people. Delegation is a way to pass down your hands-on work *and* manage, develop and empower people at the same time. It doesn't save actual time but it does give you double results from the same time investment.

It'll give you a buzz – honest!

I defy you not to be excited by seeing the light come on in their eyes when they've suddenly stopped judging themselves and started wondering and accepting. I defy you not to enjoy seeing the satisfaction on their faces when they've stretched themselves and been successful. And I defy you not to be proud when your work with them has resulted in their raising the bar of their performance standards to a permanent new height. I've spent many years managing change but the ones that have lasted haven't been the new policies, strategies, procedures and systems because new brooms sweep clean. They've been the behaviour changes.

It's a great vehicle for change

When you delegate, you elevate one task out of all the tasks your team member does and label it special because they're doing part of your job. Because of that, you get the excuse to use it as a vehicle to surface assumptions and beliefs in ways you don't get the chance to do in the normal course of managing. And you get to use it as a vehicle for changing the way you and your team member relate to each other and work together. Day-to-day management for overworked managers is usually about breadth – managing performance across a wide range of tasks, never having the time to follow one of your team member's tasks through from start to finish to really understand how they work. But delegation – investing in a team member so they can take on part of your work – is a depth issue. That is both its challenge and its reward.

It improves your employability

We all know someone who's been in the same job for many years, who was competent when they started but who hasn't kept up with the demands of the job as it's grown. Competence isn't something you achieve and then relax about: the goalposts are shifting all the time and it's easy to lose your edge. Real people management skills are at a premium, valued everywhere and can't be substituted with a qualification. Delegation improves all your people management skills.

It teaches you about people . . . and yourself

If this book has shown one thing, I hope it's that you won't get very far by seeing people as one-dimensional. The more you accept the inherent complexity of people and relationships, the more you'll see that understanding the people you work with is the key to effective performance. When you delegate, you create a different dynamic to the one that operates when your team member is doing their normal job. And in observing, taking part in and reflecting on that dynamic, you have a great opportunity to learn about yourself, your team member and the way you manage.

Above all, it teaches you to listen to your intuition, your fears, yourself

Intuition is a much underrated skill. I'm a talker (you've probably guessed that already) which doesn't predispose me to being a good listener. I find it easier to listen if I'm really concentrating and listening for anything that feels 'off'. Over the years I've added a lot of things to the

Intuition is a much underrated skill.

list of what I listen for and it's become a really helpful general management early warning radar system. Things like:

- Sweeping generalizations
- Examples of either/or thinking (I'm into the synergy of both/and thinking)
- Signs of someone's RAS at work ignoring counter evidence
- Simple solutions that don't recognize the complexity of the problem
- The things that people seem to overreact to
- People proposing solutions to problems without having identified the root cause
- People seeing only one way of looking at something (an event or person)
- People judging without having challenged their interpretation
- People making assumptions and labelling them facts
- Excessive certainty.

This isn't the whole list but it's already very long. Imagine having to listen to someone and consciously run everything they say against that list of possibilities? But I don't do it consciously. I started out consciously listening for one 'off' thing and when that became second nature (unconscious competence) I added another . . . and another. Now, I trust my intuition to notice the 'off' stuff for me. If you listen to your intuition, accept where you and your team members are coming from, and work with who people are . . . you'll be a great delegator and a great manager.

Appendix 1

Towards a way of managing for the new era

The beliefs that help me make sense of my world and the people in it, including me

Beliefs come before action – and inaction

Columbus had to believe the earth was round before he could set sail to prove it, and the same applies to us in everything we do.

People do what makes sense – even when you can't tell from their results

How many times have you reacted to someone's actions with 'But that doesn't make any sense'? We can believe human beings are irrational, or we can believe they do what makes sense but that everyone's 'sense' is different. It's easier to make sense of what people are doing if we stop thinking our logic is *the* logic. Have you ever wondered why you did something that got the opposite effect to what you wanted, even though you knew all along what would happen?

If we were conscious of everything we know, our logic would be clearer to us

Sometimes, a new experience that has similarities to an earlier experience will trigger something from the vast store of experiences we keep in our subconscious. When we do this with people, it's prejudice – literally prejudging them based on previous experience that might or might not be relevant. Have you ever taken an instant dislike to someone, then, when you got to know them, liked them? What triggered your initial response? Did they remind you of someone else you didn't like?

Our subconscious mind alerts us through our intuition

When our subconscious mind wants to tell us there's something we've forgotten that's relevant to the situation we're currently in, it uses our intuition. Have you ever listened to someone saying something that sounded logical that you still felt absolutely sure was wrong yet couldn't explain how or why?

Except when it skips that step and drives us straight to a knee-jerk action

Taking an instant dislike to someone is an example of our subconscious bypassing the intuition alert stage and driving us straight to a response. When our responses don't seem logical to our conscious minds, we fear being irrational. But as I said, people always have a logic – it just isn't always a conscious logic!

We don't fail, we just achieve an intention we didn't know we had

Have you ever tried to give up a bad habit and failed? Did you blame lack of will-power? If your conscious and subconscious minds have conflicting intentions, your subconscious will win because it's stronger. What might you have to gain from not giving up your bad habit? Or what might you have to lose from giving it up?

Our needs drive our intentions and our beliefs drive our behaviour

Our beliefs tell us how to behave to meet our needs. Like everything else we've ever learned, we learn our beliefs from our experience. What are you not doing that you know you should because you believe it will be a painful experience?

Our experience is created by our subconscious

There's a lot of rubbish talked about people creating their disability, which is a hurtful mistake people make who don't realize there's a difference between an event and an experience. Have you known two people who were at the same meeting (event) to describe it so differently (experience) that it was as if they'd been to different meetings?

Which always has its own logic – even when we can't see it

One of the main functions of our subconscious is to keep us feeling sane. The lengths it will go to is probably why it's often called the creative subconscious – as in creative accounting maybe! It governs everything, from the things we notice in the first place – have you ever bought a new car only to start seeing that model everywhere you go? – to the way we interpret events to create our experience.

Our logic comes from our beliefs

My logic will make sense to you only if we both believe that the same (a) causes the same (b). If you believe that smoking causes lung cancer but I believe there's no connection, then we'll never agree on why there's rising incidence of lung cancer among people in developing-world countries who are encouraged to smoke by unrestricted advertising practices, because we'll be analyzing using different logics.

Our ingrained beliefs stem from childhood experiences of pain and pleasure

We form many of our beliefs in childhood, which is a pity because that's when we're worst equipped to interpret events. For one thing, we're dependent on our parents to meet our needs, which means we learn to associate pleasure and pain with how they react to the way we behave to get our needs met. As adults, we can say, 'Well, that's one way of looking at it, Dad, but it's not the only way', but as children, if a parent reacts like we've done a bad thing, we've done a bad thing, and that belief stays with us until something forces us to re-examine it, if it ever does. What's your most painful childhood experience? What has it taught you to believe?

We use those beliefs to interpret later experiences

As a teenager, I got to stay up past my bedtime analyzing history with my mother. And whenever I was upset about anything, she would tell me to pull myself together and try harder. I learned that brains were 'in' and emotions were 'out', and that if at first you don't succeed, try harder and never quit. For many years, I was more Mr Spock than Captain Kirk, and I genuinely believed that my worst experiences were those when I acted on my feelings, not my logic. What about those childhood beliefs you've just identified – do they still influence the way you interpret events? (For anyone concerned for my mental health, I've cracked the 'emotions are OK' thing and I'm working really hard on giving up my stubborn refusal to quit even when I'm flogging a dead horse. I'm not there yet but I'm not going to quit until I succeed. Oh dear, maybe I'm not doing as well with that one as I thought.)

And we learn to judge ourselves according to the feedback we get

My British history teacher used to give me A+ and read my essays out to the class, praising my 'delightful prose' (oh, the shame). My European history teacher used to give me C– and suggest, caustically, 'A few more facts and a little less verbiage wouldn't go amiss.' Do you have a behaviour that's admired by some and criticized by others? In judging it, whose views matter most? If you ignored what others think, how would you rate it?

But other people's judgements of us often tell us more about them than us

I bet you learned more in the last example about my history teachers than about me. What about the people who admire and criticize your behaviour? What do their judgements tell you about them?

So we need to learn to reframe

When I lived in Brixton, I saw a poster with two photographs on it – the first was a narrow-angle shot of a black man running along a crowded street with a white policeman running after him; the second was a wide-angle shot showing both the black man and the policeman chasing a third person. It was challenging people who assumed that the black man in the first shot was a criminal, rather than a plain-clothes policeman, and showing them that they were seeing what their prejudice wanted them to see, not what was there.

When is a strength a weakness? The times it doesn't work for you

Are you sceptical about the things I'm saying? Is scepticism a strength or a weakness? When someone has to anticipate negative reactions to their proposals, scepticism can be helpful. When they're responding to radical ideas from team members by dismissing them without consideration, it's probably a weakness. How we judge a characteristic often depends on what our experience of it has been. Have you found scepticism generally helpful or hindering in your experience?

Competence is often a matter of being a round peg in a round hole

I'm not saying we don't have strengths and weaknesses. I'm saying they're just a reflection of how well we fit our operating context. My favourite ever boss was widely acknowledged as a visionary, brilliant strategist and future 'youngest ever' managing director. Yet although he'd been a good enough middle manager to get promoted, there'd been nothing to indicate how exceptional he was to become. In a middle management 'implement other people's strategies' role, he was a round peg in a square hole, but in a director role, he was in his element. What were your best and worst jobs? How did your characteristics fit your best job, and how were they a mismatch in your worst job?

To get our interpretations right, we have to slow down our judging process

Taking a more neutral approach doesn't mean no judging. We need to make judgements to move forward. What worries me is the speed with which we leap to judgement and the fact that, once decided, we lay our judgements down in our subconscious, start to live by them, and forget to take them out for review. And once we've made a judgement, our RAS ensures we see only things that reinforce the rightness of it (the sanity thing again). Given these consequences, it doesn't seem unreasonable to spend a bit more time wondering and exploring before we judge.

And take the time to listen to ourselves

Whatever we're doing, we're doing two things in parallel. Our conscious mind is doing the activity and our subconscious mind is watching us do the activity, making sure our actions are in line with our intention and triggering alarm bells when they aren't. Listening to our alarm bells is the one sure way we have of staying on the right track.

It's not just characteristics that are neutral, it's events

A friend who'd been in the same job for twenty years was made redundant. He said at the time it was the worst experience of his life. Now he says it was the best thing that ever happened to him because it made him stop, take stock of his life, and think about what he really wanted to do. And now he's doing it and he is happier than ever. Did the event go from bad to good? No, his interpretation changed. It's natural to judge events quickly. It gives us closure (what a yuk word), which allows us to move on but which also stops us learning everything the event has to teach us. Have you ever had a bad experience that you later believed had been good for you?

And emotions

Speaking as a former Mr Spock, I'm fascinated when people describe emotions as bad (anger and hurt) or good (happiness and love). Emotions exist to tell us something about an event. Anger, for example, is triggered by someone breaking a rule that we live by or trampling on a value we hold dear. Assuming we've interpreted correctly, anger tells us to put something right that's gone wrong. It's not our emotions that get us into trouble, it's our autopilot responses. Have you ever used anger, in its righteous indignation form, to right a wrong?

And pre-programmes

I have a pre-programme about consultants that says they come into the organization, talk to staff, write up our ideas (the ones our managers wouldn't take seriously when we told them), present them back to our managers (who now take them seriously because they heard them from an expensive suit), and walk off with a small fortune. My autopilot response to this pre-programme involved saying as little as possible to them. Recently, though, I've worked with a number of consultants who've not fit my subconscious expectation. Pre-programmes can be valid at the time we lay them down in our subconscious minds, but times change and we forget to bring them out and check to see whether they still hold up. Do you have a pre-programme about a group of people that you formed years ago? Are you sure it's a true reflection of your current experience of that group?

And even beliefs

Do you believe in the 'do as you would be done by' golden rule? Have you heard George Bernard Shaw's riposte: 'Do not do unto others as you would they should do unto you. Their tastes may not be the same'? As someone who likes to know where I stand with people, it took me a while to realize there are people who'd rather not know – if where they're standing is a bad place. The golden rule can be helpful as a last resort with strangers (a kind of 'if in doubt, do as you would be done by'), but there's no excuse for being in doubt with your staff

– just ask them! Have you ever done as you would be done by and got short shrift?

The difference between the 'push' and 'pull' approaches to managing change

When we're consciously trying to change something (I'm trying to give up interrupting people), we're in push mode, trying hard, working from our conscious mind. When we give up trying to force change and set our intention on being different (being a better listener), and then just observe ourselves in action, we bring our subconscious mind on board and it gently 'pulls' us towards our new intention. Have you ever set your heart on something impossible, not really worked on it, but still found all sorts of help coming your way?

We need to listen to our fears

We live in a world governed by 'feel the fear and do it anyway' sound bites. Well, let's forget the twenty-first-century pop psychology culture for a moment and think about why we have a fear mechanism. Fear is part of our survival instinct, designed to prepare us for fight or flight. It's there to tell us we need to act. If we don't listen consciously to our fears, our subconscious will listen and sabotage our efforts anyway, so we might as well.

And to the people who push our buttons

For years I've been irritated by status-conscious people. It wasn't until I looked back and realized I'd left one job when the organization became open plan and I lost my office and another because some people on my level were regraded to a higher level that I discovered a status-conscious streak I'd denied for years. What irritates you in other people? When do you display the same characteristic? If you don't believe you have it, ask someone you trust whether you have it before you dismiss what I'm saying.

And to our characteristics

Most people focus on their weaknesses and take their strengths for granted. A friend of mine counted listening as a strength, so he listened more than talked in meetings. His boss (who could win an Olympic medal for talking) branded him a poor performer because he didn't make much impact. If my friend had spent more time thinking about how his listening hindered his performance, he might have done something to improve his performance in meetings. What might you do differently if you really listened to your characteristics?

And to the standards we set ourselves

We all have an internal regulator that maintains our standards at the level our subconscious mind thinks is right for us, based on our beliefs about ourselves. What are your standards on tidiness at home? Do you feel you have to tidy up when visitors are due? Or do you always tidy the mess they make as soon as they've gone? If we don't think highly of ourselves, we settle for lower standards than we're capable of, or we push ourselves to achieve perfection – either way, we feel bad about ourselves.

And to the lessons in the experience we create

I had a colleague who believed all men were sexist. Whenever they used the masculine gender as a catch-all for both sexes, she'd tell them to say 'He stroke she'! They made fun of her and she ended up with a negative experience. I preferred to have fun at their expense. I was fond of saying things like 'I'm a man of my word' and watching their reaction – which was comical. By taking their position and exaggerating it until it became funny, I made them think about language without making them feel bad about themselves and in doing so created a different experience of them.

So we can find the beliefs that help and hinder us

Sometimes our beliefs are buried so deep in our subconscious we don't even know we've got them. Looking at our experience can tell us what we believe. Remember that bad habit you failed to give up? If I asked a neutral observer, 'What must my reader believe (about themselves, others, the world at large) to have created the experience of failing to give up that bad habit?', what would they say to me?

We all have an internal cast of characters . . .

I have a friend who's a real monster at work but completely henpecked at home. Another friend runs her own company but turns into a clinging child when her partner is going away on business. And a middle-aged friend who has a 'rebellious teenager' streak who likes to drink twelve pints on a Friday night even though he can't take his drink like he used to. I have a 'repressed child' character who pops out and emotes at people when my feelings are being ignored. Who's in your cast of characters? What provokes one of them to make an appearance? Which ones do you like, and which ones do you try to ignore?

And a dark side that can shed great light on our performance

Whatever you want to call it, we all have a person we're afraid we might be but hope we're not. We have two tactics for dealing with them – if we're conscious of them, we hide them by wearing masks.

If we're not conscious of them, we project them on to other people.

> We're **projecting** when we see in others some 'thing' (a thought, belief, characteristic or whatever) that we have in ourselves but don't see and wouldn't like if we did (which is why we don't). Our subconscious wants us to be mentally healthy, which means accepting every part of us, so it keeps showing us the bits we deny by projecting them on to other people – the ones who push our buttons. That person usually has the 'thing' in a small way, enough of a hook to hang our projection on, but not enough to justify our reaction. One of the best ways of knowing that you're projecting is when the person who pushes your buttons doesn't do it with others. That's when you know your reaction is telling you more about you than the person you're reacting to.

What characteristics don't you like about yourself? What masks do you wear to cover them up? How do your masks help you? How do they hinder you? Who gets to you in ways they don't get to other people? Which characteristic of yours might you be projecting on to them?

And coping strategies – though some work better than others

How do you cope with criticism? Do you get angry and defensive, or do you listen politely and then ignore it or feel hurt or rush to explain yourself or criticize the person right back or sulk for a few days then do something about it? If you listen, take on board what's useful, ignore the rest, and feel good towards the person doing the criticism, I probably picked the wrong example for you. I'd like to meet you, though, as I've never met anyone who doesn't use a coping strategy for criticism.

> A **coping strategy** is a pattern of behaviour that we use repeatedly as a defence against things we fear we can't cope with. They're habits and, like everything else, can be helpful or hindering depending on the situation, the use you make of them, and the effect they have.

What kinds of situations do you not like dealing with? What coping strategies do you use? They protect you, but do they have negative effects?

We influence others by acting out our subconscious expectations

My former colleague acted out her subconscious expectation of men being sexist through her attitude and behaviour, and their subconscious responded to what she was giving out. Many organizations have so many rules that they create a subconscious expectation that managers should act like parents and treat their staff like children. As an adult, I don't expect anyone to check whether I've cleaned my teeth, so how come at work we spend so much time checking the work of our staff? The more we act like parents, the more we are acting out our subconscious expectation that our staff will act like children, and the more we will create that subconscious expectation in them. No wonder we don't get excited by the prospect of empowerment programmes. If you empower children, it's all freedom and no responsibility. How do you treat the people you manage? Do you trust them to get on with the task or check up on them all the time?

And they let us – by transferring their power to us

In an organizational hierarchy, people tend to act on their subconscious expectations about authority and power. So, staff expect the manager to know the answers and, in doing so, give away their power and help sustain parent/child relationships.

We also influence by the way we reward and sanction the responses we get

I once knew a woman who could win medals for red-penning reports. Whenever one of her team wrote a report that didn't read well, instead of giving it back to them to rewrite or coaching them, she rewrote it herself. What do you think her team members were learning? What do you do when someone produces a poor-quality piece of work? We don't just reward poor performance, we punish good performance. I know someone who gives all his rush jobs to the person he trusts most. Some reward! What happens in your organization to managers who do good work?

What we focus on expands – so we need to choose carefully

When I wanted my direct reports to improve the way they managed their teams, I started asking them questions about their people management at our reviews for learning. It was amazing how much more they had to report as the months went by. Have you noticed that the better you become at something, the more of it you do? The same thing happens when we focus on our fears. They expand and our subconscious thinks our intention is to avoid the fear becoming a reality.

We can't solve problems with the same beliefs that created them

One of my team had to design a fifteen-day training programme, which more than 3000 managers would be attending. He said it couldn't be done as with those numbers it would take years. It turned out he was thinking about training people in groups of twelve. I suggested we think about the problem not as training but as event management and we ended up with a conference-style approach that allowed us to train 200 managers at a time in a large venue with lots of facilitators. When was the last time you were stuck? What part of your thinking had to change to allow you to move forward?

And we can't change behaviour until we've changed the beliefs that underpin it

Behaviour is so influenced by beliefs there's no point trying to change behaviour. All that happens when we do is we set up a clash between our conscious mind (which is managing the new behaviour) and our subconscious mind (which is trying to keep us sane by getting us to continue behaving in accordance with our beliefs). Think about a bad habit you've successfully given up. What beliefs had to change before you could give it up?

It's our unquestioned beliefs that lead to autopilot behaviour

Our bad habits tell us a lot about the beliefs we need to question. Think back to that bad habit you're trying to get rid of. What were the underlying beliefs? How long have you held them (how far back does your bad habit go)? How many times during that time have you reviewed them to see if they still hold true?

Asking the right questions transforms behaviour by transforming beliefs

Thinking is simply the process of asking ourselves questions and answering them. The trick to good-quality thinking is asking the right questions. I did a course with some twenty-year-olds. We had one lecture with a different case study every week. The lecturer shouted out the questions and we'd shout back with the answers. Everyone thought they could analyze a case study because they could answer the questions. But the lecturer asked different questions for each case study and the trick to analyzing the case studies was in knowing the right questions to ask – but no one was focusing on learning from his questioning skill. Have you ever argued with someone and been unable to change their mind, only to find that when you stopped arguing and started asking them questions they changed their own mind?

If we want to create positive experiences, we have to sweat the small stuff

People don't judge us on the big things; they judge us on their experience of us. We are much less about our major triumphs and disasters and much more about the person we show ourselves to be in those small moments of choice that happen countless times a day. Sweating the small stuff means thinking of the effect you want to achieve and the consequences of your actions before you make choices so that you make your choices – you don't let your choices make you. What makes you decide whether you admire someone?

And get off autopilot on to manual

Just because our brains like being on autopilot doesn't mean we should let them. People aren't machines. Press the key on the computer keyboard that says T, and T is what you'll get every time. Speak to the same person in the same way two days running and, if their mood or circumstances are different, you will get a different response on day two than you got on day one. Does this tie in with your experience?

Appendix 2

Questions for a brain dump

Triggering all your knowledge about a task

I deliberately hold my list in alphabetical order rather than sorting them into related issues so that I stay in right-brain mode. If I can't answer a question straightaway, I leave it and go back to it later.

- *Activities*   What kinds of activities are involved in this task?

- *Challenges*   What will be the hardest part?

- *Change issues*   What should be happening and what do we want to happen? What is the gap between what is happening and what should be happening?

- *Checkpoints*   When are the critical points in the process where I need to take stock of the situation?

- *Consequences*   What knock-on effects will there be, and on what?

- *Constraints*   What rules and procedures affect the operation of this task?

- *Context*   What else is happening in the organization that affects this task? What effect does the external (legal, political, social, economic, technological, etc.) environment have on the task itself or the way it's done?

- *Customers* Who will use the outputs? Who is next in the supply chain for this task (including other employees) and who is the end customer?

- *Expectations* What is supposed to be happening at each point in the process?

- *Implementation* What issues do we need to bear in mind when we come to implement the results?

- *Measures* What indicators (quantitative and qualitative) are needed to know if we achieved what we set out to achieve?

- *Milestones* What are the key achievements and interim deadlines during this task?

- *Monitoring* What radar system do we need to ensure we know what's happening and can pick up any blips?

- *Outcomes* What results are we trying to achieve?

- *Outputs* What do we have to produce to achieve the outcomes?

- *Parameters* What authority do we have and what do we have to refer up? Whom do we have to report back to?

- *Purpose* Why, ultimately, does the organization want this task done? If feedback indicates we need to produce a different set of outputs and change the outcomes, what is it that holds the task constant, among all the variables?

- *Quality* What would constitute a quality output?

- *Responsibilities* Who else has responsibility for delivering this task? Who should be doing what?

- *Resources* What resources do we need to do this task?

- *Risks* What could go wrong? What are our fears and what are they telling us?

- *Sponsor* Who is the originator of the task? What do they want? How will we know if they've got what they want?

- *Stakeholders* Who else is involved? Who are the impact and interest groups? What are their agendas and hot buttons? What do we need to do to manage our relationships with them?

- *Subject* What is the task about? What kind of subject is it? What's its history/background?

- *Success criteria* What has to happen for this task to be completed successfully?

- *Sustainability* What do we need to do to ensure the results are sustainable?

- *Task process* What do we need to do? What do other people need to do? How can we get everyone to do what they are supposed to do?

- *Timescales* What are the deadlines?

- *Validation* How will we know we chose the right destination in the first place? How will we be able to evaluate whether the outputs have delivered the outcomes?

- *Values* How are we going to behave in producing these outputs and achieving these outcomes? What's important about the way things are handled?

- *Verification* How will we know if we've produced what we were supposed to produce? How will we know if the outputs meet the specification?

Appendix 3

From strengths and weaknesses to characteristics

Getting into neutral to exploit all the possibilities

One of the concepts that's most prevalent in traditional management thinking is that of strengths and weaknesses. I know how hard it can be to break out of that kind of thinking so I've included some examples showing how to reframe strengths and weaknesses into characteristics that help in some cases and hinder in others and how to give them more neutral labels if they are needed.

Strengths

- *Creative*   This can be a help when it comes to problem solving and generating new ideas. However, it can hinder when it means the person sees change as the answer to everything or when they start things but lose interest in seeing them through.

- *Optimistic*   This can help people to see the positive side of a bad event but it can hinder when the person doesn't anticipate potential negative consequences.

Weaknesses

- *Laziness*   Because the word 'laziness' has only negative connotations, I reframe it as 'a dislike of wasting energy'. In fact, it can actually help when it means the person is always on the look-out for efficiencies that will save time. But it can hinder when the risk of wasting energy stops them trying something that might not pay off.

- *Arrogance*   This word also has primarily negative connotations so I reframe it as 'supreme self-belief' because (provided it's backed up by actual talent and not delusional) it can help the person keep going during very difficult problems. However, it can hinder the person when it means they use it to justify never preparing for anything.

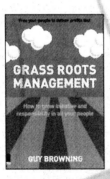

OTHER BOOKS TO MAKE YOU BETTER...
Management Skills

Fast Thinking Manager's Manual
Working at the speed of life
Ros Jay
0 273 65298 2

This essential manual gives clever tips and vital information to make the best of your last minute preparation. You'll look good. They'll never know.
The Fast Thinking Manager's Manual; it is big and it is clever.

The 90-Minute Manager
Business lessons from the dugout
David Bolchover & Chris Brady
0 273 65613 9

Football managers lead high-talent teams under intensely stressful conditions, where every action is open to scrutiny. Just like today's business environment. Time to learn the lessons from the best and the worst at the ultimate talent-management game.

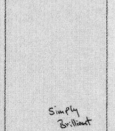

Simply Brilliant
The competitive advantage of common sense
Fergus O'Connell
0 273 65418 7

The world is full of smart, experienced, skilled, brilliant people. However, many people – even smart ones – are lacking a set of essential skills that when pulled together can be termed 'common sense'. This book provides a set of principles to make the bright better.

If you wish to find out more about any of these titles visit us at:

www.business-minds.com